r·

Lessons Learned

Lessons Learned:
The Anneliese Michel Exorcism

The Implementation of a Safe and Thorough
Examination, Determination, and Exorcism of
Demonic Possession

REVEREND BISHOP JOHN M. DUFFEY

WIPF & STOCK · Eugene, Oregon

LESSONS LEARNED: THE ANNELIESE MICHEL EXORCISM
The Implementation of a Safe and Thorough Examination, Determination and
Exorcism of Demonic Possession

Biblical quotations are from the New Revised Standard Version

Wipf & Stock
An Imprint of Wipf and Stock Publishers
199 W. 8th Ave., Suite 3
Eugene, OR 97401

www.wipfandstock.com

ISBN 13: 978-1-60899-664-3

Manufactured in the U.S.A.

For Anneliese and others

Exorcism is directed at the expulsion of demons or to the liberation from demonic possession through the spiritual authority which Jesus entrusted to his Church. Illness, especially psychological illness, is a very different matter; treating this is the concern of medical science. Therefore, before an exorcism is performed, it is important to ascertain that one is dealing with the presence of the Evil One, and not an illness.

—Catechism of the Catholic Church, §1673

Contents

Illustrations

Author's Disclaimers

1. Although the author has spent a great deal of time and effort in the collection of verifiable facts, there always remains the possibility that something was overlooked in analysis. Therefore, the author does not, in any way whatsoever, present any of his conjectures, assumptions, presumptions, inferences, opinions, or conclusions as being of absolute fact about any particular person, organization, group, historical status, event, condition, situation, or family named in this work. The reader is strongly advised to conduct his or her own research and reach his or her own conclusions and opinions regarding the incidents and materials covered in this work.

2. Any and all statements, opinions, descriptions, and inferences made by the author regarding the Michel family (Anna Michel, Anneliese Michel, Barbara Michel, Gertrud Michel, Joseph Michel, and Roswitha Michel); the Roman Catholic Church (and all subdivisions thereunder), particularly Father Arnold Renz, Father Ernst Alt, Father Herrman, Father Rodewyk, Reverend Bishop of Wurzburg Josef Stangl; clerical or administrative members of any independent Catholic Church; William Blatty; Maria Burdich; Thea Heinz; Dr. Martin Kehler; Dr. Lenner (therapist to Anneliese Michel); Dr. Siegfried Lüthy; Malachi Martin; Dr. Packhauser; Dr. M. Scott Peck; Dr. Reichelt; or Dr. Vogt are presented solely as opinions and conclusions drawn on limited factual information and are not presented by the author as absolute or partial fact or with absolute certainty regarding factuality. The reader is strongly advised to conduct his or her own research and to draw his or her own conclusions independent of any influence or aid from this literary work.

3. The Reformed Catholic Church of North America (RCCNA) is an independent Christian church that is not, in any way, affiliated with or under the direction of the Roman Catholic Church or controlled by the Vatican and its worldwide subordinate leadership. His Excellency, Bishop John M. Duffey, the author, is an ordained and consecrated bishop in the RCCNA and is not a Roman or Orthodox Catholic clergyman and does not represent himself to be one, either.

4. Laws quoted by the author come from *Criminal Law: Model Penal Code*, by Markus Dubber, published by Foundation Press in 2002, and they are limited U.S. state and federal civil statutes. The reader is advised to conduct his or her own legal research for accurate statutory and case law regulation information. The author is not responsible for the reader's misinterpretation or misunderstanding of criminal and civil laws as discussed in this book. The laws quoted and the comments made by the author are not, in any way or form, intended to be legal advice, nor is it presented as legal advice by the author. Some of the things recommended in this work may be statutorily prohibited by international, national, state, or local governments, and the reader is warned and advised to ensure what he or she does is lawful before acting.

Preface

IN FEBRUARY OF 2008, I opened up the old laptop and looked to see what was available for instant play on Netflix. Being an avid horror movie fan I saw a title that read *The Exorcism of Emily Rose*. Although I like horror movies and even favor zombies, I have been ever reluctant to watch demonic films. Strangely, this title had me utterly intrigued, and so I decided to watch it with popcorn and a pillow in hand to hide behind.

I was poised and ready to duck behind my fluffy shield when the movie started. I expected something like the well-known possession movie, *The Exorcist*. Surprisingly, I was presented with a criminal trial that flashed back to the past in order to describe a young lady who was suspected by the medical community of having epilepsy and by the Catholic world as being demonically possessed. It was like watching a splice between *Matlock* and *The Omen*. What an incredible story, I thought to myself.

The real surprise came when I discovered that the movie was based on a real event. It took a few minutes for me to pull my jaw back as I contemplated the idea that a priest would be put on trial for attempting to exorcise demons from a clearly possessed girl. It was tragic that she died, but something I saw as unforeseeable and unavoidable at the time (knowing only what the movie presented). I had sympathy for the girl and the priest in that case and felt strongly compelled to look further into the facts. I cannot really explain why the feeling to investigate was so strong, but it certainly was. I sought out as much information as possible.

THE CASE OF ANNELIESE MICHEL

I was able to quickly determine that the real story was a case that took place in Klingenberg, Germany, between 1968 and 1976. It involved a young girl named Anneliese Michel who had died on July 1, 1976, after a series of exorcism rituals that extended for months. At twenty-three, Anneliese Michel had many years left to live and a cumulative education that was soon to lead to a teaching degree. Her body was examined by a physician who refused to issue a death certificate for natural causes. The physicians examining her body noted that she was emaciated, dehydrated, and had bruises around the eyes, upon the face, and throughout her body, especially on her arms, wrists, and hands.[1] At the time of her death this once beautiful young lady was a withered, hideous, and pitiful looking creature. No priest, in his right mind, would allow such a condition to progress to the point of death.

It was discovered that two priests, Fathers Alt and Renz, were performing an exorcism with the assistance of the girl's parents, Anna and Josef Michel, months prior to and just before the young Anneliese's death. None of them could explain why they did not take the girl to the hospital for treatment when she stopped eating and began to lose weight rapidly. The presence of bruising on the body was not adequately explained, either.

Because of the doctor's professional opinion that natural death could not be determined and police suspicion of neglect or abuse on the part of the parents and attending clergy, the case was further investigated. Anna Michel, Josef Michel, Father Renz, and Father Alt were all charged criminally with negligent homicide in 1978. All were found guilty of the crime by the court, and the sentences were harsher than what was requested by the prosecution.

I found and read a book entitled *The Exorcism of Anneliese Michel* by the late Dr. Felicitas Goodman, an anthropologist noted for her expertise in exorcism and the cultural experience of demonic possession. The book was originally published in 1981, very shortly after the conclusion of the negligent homicide case against the priests and the girl's parents that started in 1978. Professor Goodman's contacts with German defense attorneys and key witnesses to the criminal trial allowed her to put together a rather detailed and accurate timeline of events. Her

---

1. Goodman, *Exorcism of Anneliese Michel*, ix.

book describes the events and experiences in Anneliese's life regarding the development of symptoms, the involvement of physicians, and the involvement of the church. Much of her information comes from records provided directly to her by defense attorneys and those records of the presiding court. She also interviewed all priests, lawyers, and related persons and included that information as well.

Although Professor Goodman infers that she had no doubt that Anneliese Michel was suffering from demonic possession experience,[2] I disagree with any such position and assert that Ms. Anneliese Michel, God rest her soul, was suffering from a combination of epilepsy and mental illness. The behaviors and experiences described by Professor Goodman, if viewed objectively, clearly indicated mental illness and epilepsy rather than diabolic possession. I am a priest with the Reformed Catholic Church of North America[3] and have been since 2004. Before my ordination I was a researcher of paranormal activities involving what many might call ghosts or specters. Additionally, I have nine years of law enforcement experience, specializing in cases of domestic violence. I conclude, based on the rather extensive information available to me, that Ms. Michel was in desperate need of psychiatric and neurological treatment and was not possessed by demons.

As I read through my own research material, and the information presented by Professor Goodman's book, I became outraged at how the church handled the Klingenberg case. Even by the strict standards of the Roman Catholic Church, this case was handled in a most negligent manner. The assessment investigation alleged by the priests was incomplete and biased, where a level of removed objectivity and thoroughness is required. Their entire assessment and determination of possession was based entirely on their observations and emotions regarding the girl's condition and absent of any medical or third-party review or involvement.

The evidence also showed that the priests failed to follow the Roman ritual for exorcism and possession determination. Even whether their bishop rendered permission for an exorcism is questionable in this case. Fathers Alt and Renz, along with at least two other background priests, acted under some sort of spiritual hysteria and failed to act rea

2. Goodman, *Exorcism of Anneliese Michel*, xvii.

3. The Reformed Catholic Church of North America and the Roman Catholic Church are not affiliated.

sonably or responsibly. They certainly do bare primary responsibility for the girl's untimely death.

Anneliese's death did not have to happen, and it was not because of demonic possession, either. Her death occurred because she could neither determine reality nor make sound decisions for herself. She was completely dependent upon her parents and the two exorcists for care and comfort. In their zealousness, they completely ignored the physical needs of the allegedly possessed girl. She slowly starved to death while suffering from tremendous episodes of psychosis mingled with epileptic attacks.

Had the priests followed a more objective, thorough, and ethical investigation, they would have concluded the same thing I have. That conclusion is that Anneliese Michel was not suffering from possession but rather a combination of mental illness and a condition of the brain known as epilepsy. Instead of performing an exorcism, they could have referred the young lady to neurologists and psychiatrists for treatment and performed a Sick Call Mass or blessing for her in the home or in the hospital. Her symptoms did not match those listed for possession but certainly did match those for episodes of schizophrenic psychosis. The priests chose to ignore this and went directly into the exorcism.

I discovered that one of the priests, Father Alt, believed that he was psychic and could tell if a person had an illness or a demon.[4] That alone dumbfounded me. Is this why all of the doctors were ignored, the investigation was haphazard, and the exorcism went on for months without regard for the girl's physical condition?

THE INTERSECTION OF DEMONOLOGY AND PSYCHOLOGY

In 1830, Sir Walter Scott, a famous writer and poet, wrote a series of letters to a dear friend that discussed the topic of demonology. These letters were later transcribed from his natural script and published by General Books in 2010 under the title *Letters on Demonology and Witchcraft*. Psychology was in its absolute infancy at that time. But, in examining his letters, the concept of mental illness and mass hysteria are certainly discussed not as possibilities but as certainties of human individual and social behavior. I am fascinated by this, as Sir Walter Scott, though a

4. Goodman, *Exorcism of Anneliese Michel*, 44–48.

well-educated man, was not academically or professionally focused on human behavior and was able to independently identify mental conditions and experiences such as mass hysteria, schizophrenic psychosis, and even depression-induced psychosis before the conditions were officially named by the likes of Freud and Jung.

If the educated classes of 1800s Europe had already begun to examine and identify mental and physiological conditions that have profound impact on reality's perception by human beings, then why have the Roman and other churches failed to endeavor toward enlightenment of the same caliber? Was it superstition? Was it fear of lost social stature or power? Why did the churches of the time resist these discoveries and strive to suppress their dissemination? Perhaps tradition and the erroneous concept of infallibility is the culprit of hindered spiritual progress in Christendom.

To this date, there are no modern written approaches to the process of determining demonic possession and the process of ethically and safely performing exorcism rituals. The most detailed document regarding exorcism available can be found in volume 2 of the *Roman Ritual*. Unfortunately, this rite was originally written when medical and mental health sciences were nonexistent or in extremely primitive forms. Thus, it does not, and didn't during the exorcism of Anneliese Michel, have any concrete approaches in the evaluation of suspected possession that included medical and mental evaluations combined with spiritual evaluations.

I do believe that Satan, along with his hundreds of thousands of demons, exists. I also believe that they exist in a dual-dimensional means that allows for both a physical and spiritual existence. But, I further realize that diseases of the body and mind simultaneously exist and that their symptoms are quite similar to the effects of possession on a human body. Thus, I stress that it is of utmost importance to have a clear and absolute understanding of the two conditions so as to assist the afflicted individual in the most appropriate and effective manner without unnecessarily endangering him or her.

I understand, as a member of the clergy, that I and every other minister in Christendom have a responsibility to ensure both the physical and spiritual wellbeing of the faithful who come to us for healing. Members of the clergy play a very important religious and social role, and that duty should not be taken lightly or abandoned in some fever of hysteria or overzealousness. Therefore, one of the goals of this book is to remind the clergy, especially those who practice the Christian faith, that we are responsible for what happens to those placed in our charge or who have placed themselves in our care for healing. We must recognize that there are limits and boundaries—where the domain of spirituality ends, medical science continues. Let us not blur the two and injure those whom we honestly and sincerely seek to heal and help.

The church is no fossil, long dead and filled with cold stone, but a living, breathing body of faith and praise to the glory, majesty, and energy of the Lord, God Almighty. The church is not a building or even a series of buildings but rather the people who have come to together in acceptance and praise of Jesus Christ, the Word made flesh. The church is a living, breathing organism whose spirit is of Christ but whose organs are of humanity. Thus, as humans err, so too does the church. It is the compassion and everlasting love of God that allows the church, God's people, to erect themselves from the fall and learn as it continues forward in the light of the Holy Spirit. To err is human, to ask forgiveness is humility, to be absolved is of the divine, and to endeavor to prevent repeating the error is responsibility. Let us all learn from our mistakes and become closer to our Lord, Jesus Christ.

IMPLEMENTING A SAFE AND THOROUGH EXORCISM

It is the Anneliese Michel exorcism case that prompted me to write this book. I believe that it is absolutely vital that priests, ministers, and demonologists of all faiths and belief systems follow a standardized, professional, thorough, and safe means and method to evaluate suspected cases of possession, determine actual possession, and to conduct an exorcism ritual that ensures the safety and wellbeing of every participant, especially the alleged victim of possession. It is essential to explore the Klingenberg case (another name for the Anneliese Michel exorcism case) and for ministers to know that a misdiagnosed possession or negligent application of an exorcism ritual can result in very tragic and deadly results.

This book examines the Anneliese Michel case as an example of poor evaluative investigation that led to misdiagnosis of possession and negligent application of the exorcism rite. It then moves into an in-depth discussion of some of the chief medical and mental health diseases and disorders that can mimic the signs of possession and confuse an investigating member of the clergy or other form of exorcist. Finally, it moves into discussing a safe, ethical, and effective approach to the performance of an exorcism rite.

Written primarily for clergy and members of the Christian faith (Protestant, Roman Catholic, New American Catholic, and Orthodox) this book certainly is applicable to other faiths as well. What has often been forgotten by exorcists in the past is that the battle against the Dark One takes place not just in the spiritual realm but in the physical realm, too. Failing to care for the subject's physical and emotional needs during the process of exorcism is equally as dangerous as ignoring the spiritual needs.

Acknowledgments

I would like to give special thanks to the following:

1. The Father, the Son, and the Holy Spirit; the holy Trinity in its individual and combined elements has filled me with insight, enlightenment, compassion, love, clear vision, faith, and determination to both expose and offer cure to a sore in the history of Christendom.

2. My lovely wife, Jennifer Duffey, whose boundless love and support kept me going when I thought I could go no further. I give thanks also for my two lovely children, Heather and John II, who have rendered unconditional love, admiration, and support, that surely I would die without. I love them one and all and thank God for these most precious of all divine gifts.

3. My mother-in-law, Margie Bennett, whose faith in Christ, love for humanity, compassion for others, and unending charity has, like a beacon of light in the dark abyss, drawn me closer to God and enhanced my appreciation for all of God's holy works.

4. My mother, Nana Duffey, whose endless love and support delivered me through the worst of times with unharmed faith in God and humanity.

5. Mrs. Henry and Mrs. White, my ninth and eleventh grade English teachers, who were convinced that my writing skill would not develop beyond that of a Neanderthal. Thank you for not giving up on me as your hard work and patience have paid off.

Abbreviations

ADHD	Attention deficit/hyperactivity disorder
ADP	Adrenal dysfunction psychosis
CNS	Central nervous system
DSMMD	*Diagnostic and Statistical Manual of Mental Disorders*
EEG	Electroencephalogram
EPA	Extraphysiological ability
IREF model	Investigate, review, exorcise, and follow up
RCCNA	Reformed Catholic Church of North America.
PTSD	Post-traumatic stress disorder
OCD	Obsessive compulsive disorder
TBI	Traumatic brain injury
UPA	Ultraphysical ability

PART 1

Historical Information Regarding Anneliese Michel

Man's insanity is heaven's sense.

—Herman Melville, *Moby Dick*

1

The Life of Anneliese Michel

1.1 CHILDHOOD

THE INFANT ANNELIESE MICHEL was born to Anna and Josef Michel on September 21, 1952, in Leiblfing, Germany. All who viewed her agreed that she was a very beautiful and healthy girl, and the parents were indeed proud. Baby Anneliese was christened into the Roman Catholic faith in accordance with the local Bavarian customs of the time.

Anneliese was one of several daughters born to Anna and Josef Michel. Her older sister, Martha Michel, died at the age of eight due to complications related to kidney disease. Anneliese was then one of the oldest children living in the house, and her mother expected a great deal more than she may have been able to cope with.

Anneliese's father, Josef Michel, was a veteran of World War II and barely managed to survive fighting for the German army on the Eastern front. He fought his way westward in order to surrender to United States and British forces and would often tell young Anneliese stories about his experiences in the war. One story involved his marching in the snow without boots and then finding a pair of Russian boots in the snow after praying for God's help. This story was one of Anneliese's favorites, and she would often ask her father to retell it.

Joseph Michel has been described as nice and caring toward his children but also of being emotionally vacant and out of touch with his emotions. This may have been the result of having survived a very bloody and brutal war. It was quite common for veterans of World War II to be emotionally vacant and hard. In all accounts he seemed to care a lot about his daughters but lacked an ability to effectively show it or emotionally nurture them.

Anneliese's mother, Anna Michel, was an extremely religious and strict parent. Both Anneliese and her sisters described Anna as being a suffocating and overbearing mother. Anneliese and her sisters were controlled in almost every aspect of their lives. They were strictly forbidden to interact with members of the opposite sex and would not even be allowed to go to a female friend's house if that female friend had a brother. None of the children were allowed to develop individually or to interact in social environments that would have allowed them to develop healthy adaptation and coping mechanisms in times of stress and disruptive change. The girls weren't even allowed to go dancing at special school events.

What was to be worn, what was to be read, what was to be discussed, and manners of behavior were strictly dictated by both of Anneliese's parents. Punishments for emoting or expressing feelings that were contrary to the strict and quite unreasonable standards of the family were harsh. Normal developmental interests in issues of sex and sexuality were suppressed, and those who expressed curiosity or developmental interests were quickly scorned and told not to do or speak of things that would make them look promiscuous. All of the children were expected to sacrifice their own emotional health and individuality for the primary benefit of their mother, Anna Michel.

Later, Anneliese would meet with a psychotherapist named Dr. Lenner who saw the young girl as having a classic case of neurosis, which was rooted in her dysfunctional family life. Dr. Lenner noted that Anneliese's neurosis slowly manifested itself from having a father who didn't understand her and a mother for whom she had intense hatred.[1] The suspected use of holy objects and prayers as punishments and control mechanisms certainly can be seen as contributing factors for Anneliese's later development of contempt for any Catholic icon or practice.

In 1965, at the age of thirteen, young Anneliese was enrolled at the Dalberg-Gymnasium in Aschaffenburg, Germany. She was excited and liked taking the train into Aschaffenburg from her home in Klingenberg

1. Goodman, *Exorcism of Anneliese Michel*, 53.

each day. Perhaps it offered her a bit of cherished freedom from her mother and the house. She was a very good student and excelled in her studies, especially Latin. Up until then she was a very happy, engaging, and playful person. She was healthy and enjoyed athletics. But, this was soon to change drastically when she experienced her first of many symptoms that would come to be medically identified as epileptic seizures and spiritually misidentified as demonic possession.

1.2 HISTORY OF SYMPTOMS

Anneliese was sixteen years old and had just started her 1968–69 school year when she blacked out for a moment during class. She appeared to be in some sort of trancelike state to her friends sitting next to her. They all asked her if she was OK, and she stated that she was fine and was probably tired from all of her studying.[2] She really had no idea what had just happened to her.

That night, sometime around midnight, Anneliese awoke suddenly. She experienced a sensation of something heavy pressing down on her combined with a sort of paralysis that rendered her unable to move or yell for help. She struggled desperately to breath. The terrified girl lost bladder control and felt warm urine running across her legs.[3] The episode didn't last very long and ended as quickly as it started. She quickly got up, cleaned herself and changed the bedding. She didn't awaken her parents right then but did discuss the matter with her mother the next morning. The experience was absolutely terrifying to her.

After this event, everything seemed to return to normal for Anneliese Michel. She began to learn how to play tennis, and final examinations were approaching. As with any other normal teenage girl, she worried about school, interacted with her classmates, and spoke about boys with the other girls. She did not have any other experiences until August of 1969.

Almost a year after her first episode, Anneliese again experienced the strange blackout in class. That, like the first incident, was followed by a late night awakening with the sensation of something heavy pressing down on her. She also experienced the strange paralysis and un-

2. Goodman, *Exorcism of Anneliese Michel*, 14.
3. Goodman, *Exorcism of Anneliese Michel*, 13.

controlled urination. As with the first incident, these symptoms came and went very quickly. Again, she changed herself and the bedding and waited until morning to tell her mother about the problem she had.

Since this was the second time that Anneliese had experienced such an episode, her mother decided that it was time to take her to the family physician there in Klingenberg. Dr. Vogt performed an examination and listened to the girl describe her experiences. Based on what he heard, Anneliese was referred to a neurologist in Aschaffenburg named Dr. Siegfried Lüthy. Anneliese's mother overreacted and asked repeatedly as to what could be wrong with her Anneliese that would require a nerve doctor. She insisted that Anneliese not say a word to anyone about her being referred to a nerve doctor, as there would be gossip. Anna Michel was worried more of what the people in town and at church would think than what was truly ailing her daughter.[4]

Dr. Lüthy asked a number of questions, performed a physical examination, and ran a battery of tests. The results of his observations and tests indicated that there was nothing neurologically wrong with Anneliese. However, he did make an appointment with Anneliese for August 27, 1969, in order to perform an electroencephalogram (EEG). The results of this examination also indicated normal brainwave activity.

Although Dr. Lüthy found nothing abnormal about Anneliese's brain and neurological functioning, he did suspect that Anneliese had experienced symptoms of grand mal seizures. He indicated these suspicions during interviews with investigators on February 9, 1977. He also stated emphatically that, based on the fact that she had experienced only one previous episode a year ago, he did not prescribe any medications to treat epilepsy, seizures, or any other neurological disorder.[5]

During this same time frame Anneliese frequently complained of a sore throat, which eventually led to a tonsillectomy. She was forced to withdraw from the 1969–70 school year due to the contraction of pleurisy and pneumonia. These conditions were further complicated by a tuberculosis infection. She was confined to her bed, which was most assuredly a miserable state for the young girl.

Being isolated from friends, confined to her bed, and having to endure an unreasonably controlling and overbearing mother must have felt like a term in prison. Anneliese could not express disagreements

4. Goodman, *Exorcism of Anneliese Michel*, 15.
5. Goodman, *Exorcism of Anneliese Michel*, 15.

with her mother and was not allowed to develop individual thoughts and beliefs. Moreover, when Anneliese expressed anger or disagreement, her mother would ignore her by using loud rosary prayer. This situation undoubtedly had a profound and deep psychological impact on Anneliese. Her mother maintained absolute control over every aspect of Anneliese's life. There were no boundaries, no privacy, and no individual thoughts or emotion.

Anneliese did not show much improvement and in February of 1970 was admitted to a special hospital for children with lung diseases in Aschaffenburg. This was a significant life change that occurred outside of her control. She was taken away from a familiar environment and placed in a cold and sanitized environment with people she did not know. On February 28, 1970, she was transferred to a specialized clinic in Mittelberg, Bavaria.

Again, Anneliese found herself in a strange place with strange people. Having lived such a controlled life, her ability to adapt to such significant life changes was limited. She became more depressed, felt further isolated, and became withdrawn. To make things worse, the other children in the clinic shunned and ridiculed her. The term "snot nose" was used frequently by the children to describe Anneliese. This was probably because her reclusive nature was interpreted as being stuck-up or antisocial. This added tremendous emotional stress to her. Family visits weren't very frequent, either.

She did receive regular letters from home, however. Although disappointed that the letters read more like church sermons than relaxed and casual conversations, she was very happy to get them. It at least reminded her of home, the environment in which she was most comfortable and felt less vulnerable. Saying the rosary, a daily tradition back home, also gave her a connection to a better place.

On June 3, 1970, a Wednesday, Anneliese experienced her third terrifying episode. It was late, near midnight, when her arms became stiff and rigid; she felt the sensation of a heavy weight pressing down on her, the paralysis, and the uncontrolled urination. She made great effort to yell for help but was unable to do so until the incident stopped. Just as always, the episode ended as quickly as it began, and she finally emitted a toe curling scream that awoke everyone. By the time the nurses got to her the symptoms had vanished. She was comforted, cleaned-up, and moved to another bed.

The next morning Anneliese was bombarded by derogatory and ridiculing comments and declarations from her fellow juvenile patients.[6] Some claimed that she was crazy while others declared that she was possessed by the devil. One patient stated that Anneliese had an angry expression on her face with rigid hands that resembled a cat stretching its claws.[7] All of this served only to further isolate and humiliate the girl. She didn't understand what was happening to her, she didn't understand why it was happening to her, and she was being treated like a freak by everyone around her. The feelings of loneliness and despair must have been tremendous for her.

Not long after this experience Anneliese had an entirely different life event. While saying the rosary, Anneliese began to smell a sweet odor similar to or the same as violets. She also began to feel euphoric. She reported in her diary that sounds and colors were more vivid and she had a feeling of ecstasy. She was startled from her experience by other patients who asked her what was wrong. They pointed out to her that her hands had become rigid and outstretched, like a cat stretching its claws. They also noted that she appeared to be in some sort of trance-like state. Her euphoric feeling lasted through to the next day, and she became convinced that it was the work of the Virgin Mary.

Following this fourth experience, Anneliese was transported to a neurologist named Dr. von Haller. An EEG test was run on her, and he observed that there were irregular alpha wave patterns mixed with scattered delta and theta waves. The doctor prescribed antiseizure medication, which marked the beginning of her treatments for epilepsy.

For weeks after her rosary experience, Anneliese tried very hard to regenerate the euphoric and ecstatic experience she enjoyed so much. Each time she prayed the rosary without the experience she would rationalize that perhaps the Virgin Mary was busy helping so many others. It is important to note that she was also taking prescription antiseizure medication during that timeframe at the clinic. This seems to indicate that the medication was helping.

However, other symptoms began to manifest themselves. One evening, and for only an instant similar to the flash of a camera, Anneliese saw a grimacing face that terrified her greatly. She would later describe it as definitely being outside of her and very real. Because the first

6. Goodman, *Exorcism of Anneliese Michel*, 17.
7. Goodman, *Exorcism of Anneliese Michel*, 19.

manifestation of these faces occurred while she was praying the rosary Anneliese wrote a letter home that expressed a fear of attempting to say the rosary again. She would report being plagued by ever more frequent visions of grimacing faces for the remainder of her short life, with or without saying the rosary.

Eventually, Anneliese's heart and circulation problems, detected while she was at the sanitarium, were resolved enough for her to be discharged from the clinic and sent home. That was one of the happiest times for Anneliese, as she was clearly miserable in the clinic and eager to get back to a more comfortable setting. From the time she had started receiving medication to the time of her release, she had experienced visions of the grimacing faces several times but not the trancelike states. Medical professionals expressed suspicion that Anneliese was experiencing visual hallucinations related to epilepsy.[8]

Upon returning home, everyone immediately noticed that Anneliese's behavior and personality were remarkably different than what they were before she entered the sanitarium. Her sister, Roswitha, noted that Anneliese was irritable and unhappy all the time.[9] Outbursts of anger became more frequent and more intense as time went by. Everyone at church also began to notice the change in Anneliese. She seemed distant and moody, with a growing resentment for Roman Catholic icons and devices. Her angry outbursts would eventually grow into frequent and uncontrolled rages.

Anneliese also began to experience a return of the seizures. She would freeze in rigid postures with a contorted and angry looking face. Occasionally, a loss of bladder control accompanied the attacks. Anneliese was not on the medication she was taking at the sanitarium when these attacks resumed. These symptoms caused her mother Anna to become even more controlling, which only served to exacerbate emotional and physical problems for Anneliese.

As the first day of the 1970–71 school year approached at the Euroschule in Aschaffenburg, Anneliese became increasingly anxious. She was worried about how she would be accepted by her peers and what would be thought of her for being a year behind. Her sister, Gertrud, reassured and consoled her by saying there would be people there that

8. Dr. Lüthy, official investigatory statement, Bavaria-Germany, 1977, quoted in Goodman.

9. Goodman, *Exorcism of Anneliese Michel*, 22.

she knew. Gertrud went on to say that nobody would hold falling behind a year due to illness against her. This was comforting to Anneliese, but the stress remained high for her.

At school, Anneliese encountered a longtime friend named Maria Burdich. She was very eager to discuss her experiences with Maria, but was unable to do so as Maria showed more interest in discussing boys than strange and possibly spiritual experiences.[10] This was one of many attempts to reach out to friends for assistance in dealing with her problems. As each attempt failed, Anneliese became increasingly withdrawn and depressed. Her grades and class participation reflected this development.

It was around the beginning of the school year, when her stress levels were high and she struggled to adapt to a new social environment, that Anneliese endured another seizure. Just like all of the previous episodes, she had a momentary trancelike experience during the day followed by the sensations of a heavy weight, paralysis, breathing difficulty, and loss of bladder control. Her mother took her to a specialist in nearby Miltenberg named Dr. Reichelt who discovered some circulatory irregularities and referred Anneliese to another internist named Dr. Packhäuser. Although little is known about what the internist recommended for the circulatory condition, the doctor did write a note to Anneliese's family physician, Dr. Vogt, that expressed concern about her seizures.[11]

Anneliese was growing increasingly irritated by all of the doctor visits and the fact that little was being done to cure her. She began to bury herself in Christian literature and practice. She read many books and articles about different saints and local shrines. She was particularly fascinated by the life of Barbara Weigand. Several letters written by Anneliese to family, friends, and religious ministers seem to indicate that she identified heavily with the life of Barbara Weigand. She began to develop a belief that she was being made to suffer for a greater spiritual reason, which allowed the delusion of being chosen for a special and saintly mission to manifest in her desperate mind.

Her mother was equally desperate for her daughter to be afflicted with anything but mental illness. She remained alarmed and worried about what people would think of her for having a daughter who was

---

10. Goodman, *Exorcism of Anneliese Michel*, 26.
11. Goodman, *Exorcism of Anneliese Michel*, 27.

crazy. She simply could not deal with that reality in her life. Thea Heinz, a good friend and prominent member of the church, became sympathetic to Anna and suggested that perhaps Anneliese was suffering from demonic possession. Anna Michel latched on to this idea with feverish devotion. After all, who could blame her for a daughter who had been attacked by demons?

The ugly faces Anneliese saw suddenly became demonic entities, and her seizures became episodes of demoniacal possession. As the girl's mental condition deteriorated and her seizures became more frequent and intense, the belief that demons were tormenting her became more easily ingrained in the minds of her family, church fellows, and clergy. However, the medical community remained resolute in their belief that Anneliese was suffering from epilepsy and extreme episodes of schizophrenic psychosis.

By 1973, Anneliese was in college studying to be a teacher. That was something her mother decided was best for her. Whether or not Anneliese actually shared her mother's view is uncertain. What is certain is that her condition was considerably worse. She was struggling to pay attention in class, finish assignments, and even find the energy to get out of bed in the morning. She had contemplated suicide several times but confessed to her therapist that she did not have the courage to carry out the deed.[12] She remained severely depressed, her hallucinations were intense and frequent, and the medications didn't seem to be very effective regarding her seizures.

Between March and April of 1973, Anneliese Michel's hallucinations took another turn for the worse. She began to hear knocking sounds while in bed at night. These sounds were not heard by any of the other members of her family. Mother and daughter Michel went to see Dr. Vogt who referred them to an unknown audiologist for testing. Subsequent hearing and ear examinations revealed nothing out of the ordinary for the young lady. Strangely, after the suggestion of demonic possession was made, Anna Michel, who had earlier told Anneliese that she must have been dreaming, suddenly began to complain of hearing the sounds, too.

Anneliese would see Dr. Lüthy, the neurologist, on January 18, March 27, June 4, and June 6 of 1973.[13] He continued to monitor her

12. Goodman, *Exorcism of Anneliese Michel*, 33.

13. Goodman, *Exorcism of Anneliese Michel*, 29.

and prescribed an antiseizure medication known in Europe as Zentropil. After giving the medication time to reach full potency in the brain, Dr. Lüthy had another EEG run on Anneliese during the June 4, 1973, visit. The results of this examination indicated normal brainwave activity. According to Felicitas Goodman, author of the book entitled *The Exorcism of Anneliese Michel*, Anneliese did not discuss the visual and auditory hallucinations with the neurologist during this time frame. She would not inform Dr. Lüthy of these experiences until September of 1973.

During a meeting with Dr. Lüthy, on September 3, 1973, Anneliese stated that the devil was inside her and that a judgment of fire would be visited upon everyone. He noted that Anneliese appeared obsessed with Satan being inside her and was very disoriented, indecisive, and random in thought.[14] According to Dr. Lüthy, Anneliese was incapable of making decisions for herself at this point.[15]

Around this time, Anneliese began to see Father Ernst Alt. He had a keen interest in Anneliese's condition and was inclined to believe that she was indeed suffering from demonic possession. This member of the Roman Catholic Church also claimed to be psychic and telepathic, with a special ability to know if a person was possessed by demons or physically ill.[16] This fact is shocking to every priest, minister, and psychologist who hears of it. It is absolutely confounding that a bishop would listen to and agree with a determination of demonic possession based on psychic phenomena and telepathy. Father Alt would be described by psychiatrists in 1978 as having "an abnormal personality in the widest sense of the term. Parts of his prehistory, as he reported them, even suggest the presence of a psychosis of the schizophrenic type."[17]

Father Alt reported in a letter to Reverend Bishop of Wurzburg Josef Stangl and to his evaluating therapists that he saw visions of the living Christ. He heard a voice calling out that said "for you." Apparently the vision went away as fast as it came. Surprisingly, a lot of the things described by Father Alt that were determined to be manifestations of schizophrenic psychosis are remarkably similar to the experiences re-

14. Goodman, *Exorcism of Anneliese Michel*, 36.

15. Dr. Lüthy, official investigatory statement, Bavaria-Germany, 1977, quoted in Goodman.

16. Fr. Ernst Alt to Bishop Stangl, September 30, 1974, quoted in Goodman.

17. Goodman, *Exorcism of Anneliese Michel*, 43.

ported by young Anneliese. Considering that she was incapable of deciding for herself on even the minutest of life's details, Anneliese was very impressionable and vulnerable to suggestion. It is entirely plausible to say that Father Alt's delusions impacted and influenced Anneliese's beliefs and delusional behavior. It may have even fueled her psychosis into ever worsening states.

From the fall of 1973 through to the summer of 1975, Anneliese would visit with a Father Herrman about ten times. He was a retired priest who had more time to devote to Anneliese than her parish priest and Father Alt did. He was willing to meet with and counsel the young lady while evaluating her for telltale signs of demonic possession or molestation.

In each visit, Father Hermann and Anneliese would discuss her general life issues for about half an hour and then pray together. Often, they would pray the rosary together without incident. He reported during an investigatory interrogation in 1977 that Anneliese would often say that she was no longer herself and that she felt as though she were someone else or under the control of someone else. Additionally, he noted that she was very nice and polite while displaying no angry expressions or ill behavior towards him or holy items. Father Herrman stated that he observed nothing that indicated demonic possession or influence in Anneliese Michel. He further reported that none of the violent behavior or hateful speech that was described to him by Anna Michel manifested in any meeting he had with Anneliese.

Anneliese Michel experienced heightened stress and sadness starting on May 15, 1975, when her grandmother died. She was quite close to her grandmother, and the impact of her death was hard. Additionally, her sister Barbara was moving away to pursue a career. These changes, to which Anneliese was exceptionally sensitive and unable to cope, came at about the same time as her alleged infestation with demonic spirits named Cain, Nero, Adolf Hitler, Fleischmann, Judas, and Lucifer. Discussions over the years with Father Alt and listening to the statements of Anna Michel undoubtedly made the development of these multiple personalities, known as dissociative disorder today, more possible for Anneliese as she attempted to cope with reality. A year earlier, September 9, 1974, Anneliese told Father Alt, "I cannot cope with reality."[18]

---

18. Goodman, *Exorcism of Anneliese Michel*, 61; Anneliese Michel to Father Ernst Alt, September 9, 1974, quoted in Goodman.

It was in late 1974 that the mental breakdown occurred. Anneliese lost all touch with reality and began to behave as different personalities. She switched from one personality to another rapidly and randomly, her hallucinations became more frequent and intense, and she was unable to tell the difference between the realm of reality and that of the imagination. Anneliese would display intense fits of anger between legitimate epileptic attacks. The young lady was beginning to enter a very serious mental health crisis.

Throughout 1975, Anneliese would be visited numerous times by Father Alt and Father Arnold Renz. Both observed Anneliese and determined that she was not mentally ill but possessed by demons. They followed no standardized investigative process and based all of their determinations on a clearly subjective perspective and a belief that Father Alt was psychic. The records kept were recordings of the exorcism rituals. Undoubtedly, those involved saw value in tapes that could inspire a movie like *The Exorcist*. Very little attention was paid to understanding Anneliese's mental and medical health history, no time was taken to evaluate her home life and its developmental impact on Anneliese, and no time was spent on understanding what demonic possession truly was.

Sunday, August 3, 1975, was the day that Anneliese underwent the first of many exorcism rituals. Father Alt had received permission verbally, so he reported, from Bishop Stangl to perform a small exorcism and not the full, or great, exorcism. Father Alt reported that Anneliese seemed to feel and act better following the ritual but remained concerned that further demonic molestations may occur. It cannot be determined as to whether or not he planted any suggestions of these doubts with Anneliese.

Bishop Stangl issued a formal written authorization for Father Alt to perform an exorcism on Anneliese Michel. The bishop relied entirely on what Father Alt told him and did not demand documentation concerning the girl's mental health and other issues, which would show her to be mentally unstable and not possessed. The first full exorcism rite was scheduled to take place on September 24, 1975. Father Renz met with Anneliese and her parents, Josef and Anna Michel, and did not see anything that indicated demonic possession.[19]

---

19. Goodman, *Exorcism of Anneliese Michel*, 93.

From September of 1975 to the day of her death on July 1, 1976, Anneliese would undergo exorcism after exorcism, each of which would last for hours. She lost her interest in eating and began to literally waste away. Every day, her parents and the priests would see that she had grown weaker and skinnier, yet they never once contacted a physician or had her transported to a hospital. In fact, they kept it all very secret and told no one of what they were doing. None of the exorcism sessions managed to improve her condition.

Instead of reevaluating the situation and determining that Anneliese was not the victim of demonic possession but was in fact quite mentally ill, the priests and her family continued with the rituals. There is an entry in the *Roman Ritual* that states that one type of possession requires fasting and deep prayer for both the victim and the exorcist.[20] Since Anneliese was claiming to be possessed by Satan, the priests and family may have denied the girl sustenance in the belief that this would drive out Satan. It would certainly explain why they did not stop and seek medical help.

Anneliese Michel, aged twenty-three years, died on July 1, 1976. Her father, Josef Michel, immediately left to get a natural causes death certificate issued under unusual rush conditions. He hadn't even taken the time to mourn the loss before seeing to the administrative issues related to his daughter's death. This almost immediately raised suspicions regarding the circumstances of the girl's death.

The examining physician utterly refused to issue a death certificate for natural causes, based on the extreme emaciation of the body and the presence of multiple wounds and contusions throughout. Anneliese Michel was extremely emaciated, had fractured teeth, both eyes blackened, and a number of bruises on the arms, wrists, and hands.[21] Dr. Martin Kehler recommended to the prosecutor's office that a full autopsy be performed on the girl.

Throughout the investigation and during the criminal trial in 1978, the bruising and other wounds observed on Anneliese's body were never fully explained by the priests or the parents. The reasoning for not getting the girl much-needed medical attention was also unexplained. What happened may never be completely known. Not addressing these

---

20. Weller, *Roman Ritual*, 2:171.

21. Dr. Martin Kehler, postmortem report on Anneliese Michel, July 1, 1976, quoted in Goodman.

questions was most likely in the interests of the defendants, as it very well could have caused a negligent homicide charge to be changed into a second- or even first-degree murder charge.

During investigative interrogations in 1977 and in documentary interviews conducted years after the 1978 trial, Father Ernst Alt claimed that the wounds were part of the stigmata.[22] However, there was very little evidence that Anneliese had actually received the stigmata. She complained of painful sensations, but the requisite wounds of the stigmata did not actually manifest on her body. They were not present on her body at the time of death, but bruises around the wrists and arm were present, which seemed to indicate forceful resistance to physical restraint rather than the stigmata.[23]

1.3 MEDICAL AND PSYCHOLOGICAL DIAGNOSIS AND TREATMENT

Throughout Anneliese Michel's short lifetime, she was examined by a plethora of physicians who ranged in specialty from general practice to psychiatry and neurology. Every one of these doctors believed that she suffered from a condition of the brain known as epilepsy. The neurologists, who were also trained in psychiatry, diagnosed a condition of either schizophrenic or manic depressive (bipolar disorder) psychosis. But, there is absolutely no doubting that the medical science community did not see anything in Anneliese's history and experiences that were outside the realm of medical science.

From the time of Anneliese's third epileptic seizure she was treated with antiseizure medications. Some worked better than others, but there was noteworthy success in these treatments. The points where Anneliese's conditions worsened are centered on major life changing or

22. The stigmata is a condition of unexplained wounds that manifests itself on people believed to have been blessed by God for their piousness. The wounds appear upon the parts of the body where the wounds of the crucifixion were sustained by Christ. The wounds are ulcerous and often bleed. The locations of the stigmata wounds are usually the palm of each hand, the top of the feet, the forehead, and the lower right side of the rib cage. The wounds are said to appear without warning or cause and may last for varying periods of time. Some people are reported to have experienced stigmata episodes numerous times in their lifetimes.

23. Dr. Martin Kehler, postmortem report on Anneliese Michel, July 1, 1976, quoted in Goodman.

stressor events. Test anxiety, especially around the time of the Arbitur, a test in the German educational system that follows the end of a student's twelfth year of study, and collegiate end-term exams, triggered many of her seizures and psychotic episodes. Changes in living arrangements and conditions also triggered epileptic and psychotic episodes. A correlation clearly exists between Anneliese's most difficult episodes and life stress levels.

During the 1970s it was believed that psychosis could be successfully treated with psychotherapy. Not as much about brain chemistry was known then, and so the immediate introduction or even consideration of antipsychotic or antidepressant medications would have been less likely to occur. Of course, this is in contrast with today, where medical science has greatly expanded its knowledge of the brain and neurochemical processes. Many of the drugs available today didn't exist in Anneliese Michel's time.

Although there were some differences between the physicians regarding the type and root causes of psychosis, there was no doubting that it was present along with epilepsy. Certainly, they saw nothing that was out of the norm for a person experiencing a very abnormal mental condition. The last thing on their minds was the need for an exorcism ritual performed by priests or that anything supernatural was involved at all in Anneliese's case. Doctors Lenner and Lüthy both testified to this during the 1977 investigation and 1978 criminal trial.

One of the most unique elements of the Klingenberg case is the fact that Anneliese Michel claimed to have been possessed by only one demonic entity and that entity was Satan. The rest were Cain, Hitler, Fleischmann (a disgraced clergyman in the local area history), Judas, and Nero. These were all humans and cannot be even remotely classified as demons. This should have been a huge red flag for the exorcists in evaluating whether this was a case of diabolic possession or mental illness. Demons possess and humans don't.

What was happening here? For many mental health professionals, each of these personalities identified a part of Anneliese. Cain killed his brother, Nero persecuted Christians, Judas was a traitor to Christ, Fleischmann was a womanizing priest of long ago, and Hitler had horrendous rage that resulted in the deaths of millions. There is sexuality, rage, and guilt described in these personas. Satan becomes a personification of her feelings of worthlessness and evil. Is it possible for these to be expressions rather than demons?

Was Anneliese struggling with her developing adulthood? It is certainly plausible to say that Anneliese felt guilty for being angry at her mother and for having sexual desires for her boyfriend, Peter. She may have had great resentment for her mother's overbearing and over-controlling behavior. She may have felt like a horrible traitor to her faith and to her mother for being angry and desirous of individuality. Anneliese had a great many emotions of anger and guilt pent up inside her and no healthy way to get them out. Were the alleged demons nothing more than personified icons of these emotions?

1.4 RELIGIOUS RATIONALIZATION, SUPERSTITION, AND SOCIAL HYSTERIA

For Roman Catholics, the devil is a very real entity that has forms in both the physical and spiritual realms. In this belief system, Satan and his demons can both walk about in their own forms or invade the bodies of unwitting humans. Unlike many Protestants, Catholics believe that demonic entities can invade the body of any person they choose regardless of the saintly or sinful nature of the targeted person.

Anneliese Michel was an avid reader of religious books and material on different saints and martyrs of the Catholic faith. She was also an excellent student of Latin; in fact, she was nearly fluent. Her studious nature allowed her to acquire a thorough understanding of ancient Roman and local history. This is especially so regarding local churches and their many priests. It is this knowledge of local church and shrine histories that allowed Anneliese to manifest many of her personalities and delusions.

Anneliese's gullibility in believing she was possessed by Fleishman is a case in point. Father Fleischmann was a long-passed priest listed in a local church's records as a womanizing drunkard who once beat a man to death.[24] He was shamed and removed from his position. After Father Ernst Alt, the self-proclaimed psychic and telepath, was transferred to the church in Ettleben, he conducted research on the church in order to

---

24. Fr. Ernst Alt, taped interview with F. D. Goodman, July 1979, quoted in Goodman; Goodman, *Exorcism of Anneliese Michel*, 106.

determine who he should go to for assistance in having repairs made. He discovered the name of a Pastor Fleischmann who served as the priest for the church during the 1500s.

For some reason, Father Alt decided to discuss this finding with Anneliese's parents in a manner that was well within earshot of Anneliese. The very next week, Anneliese was suddenly possessed by another demon named "Fleischmann." How incredibly convenient that was. It demonstrates how easily Anneliese could be given suggestion and how quickly that suggestion would be integrated into her alternate reality as an additional personality. This is a huge indicator of psychological disorder rather than demonic activity.

It was Anneliese's thorough study of Barbara Weigand, a person that the local people were hoping to see beatified by the Vatican during Anneliese's time, which allowed Anneliese to identify with the sufferings of a saintly person and believe that her own sufferings were at the order of the Virgin Mary for a great and holy purpose.[25]

Academically, Anneliese Michel was an exceptionally gifted person. Her ability to absorb and retain anything she read was extraordinary. This was especially true for subjects in which she was most interested. To believe that she did not know nor had any way of knowing about people such as Nero, Judas, Cain, and Adolf Hitler is ludicrous. She studied these people intensely through a variety of formal and informal means.

Her interest in Roman history and the Latin language would lead her to be very well exposed to the life of Nero and his persecution of Christians. He blamed Christians for all of Rome's problems and indeed hated the lot of them. Being very religious and having read the Bible many times along with additional documents on characters such as Cain and Judas made her utterly familiar with their deeds and personalities. Cain's and Judas's primary qualities somehow match a feeling or image she held of herself. Being a German raised in the recovery wake of the Nazi regime makes Anneliese quite familiar with the evils of Hitler and the many things that took place within Germany. There is no surprise in her selection of these people to represent certain aspects of her psychological troubles.

Anna Michel, Anneliese's mother, was an avid believer in the archaic belief elements of a bygone Catholic era. She was quite literally medieval about her faith and view of the church and Christ. Anna har-

25. Goodman, *Exorcism of Anneliese Michel*, 136.

bored a long-lasting and deep belief that Anneliese had been cursed by a neighbor who was jealous of not having such a beautiful baby. It is something that most people are accustomed to hearing from followers of voodoo in Haiti instead of a Catholic in Germany. Her belief in dark magic, curses, and the ever-present and lurking elements of the demonic world made many fellow Catholics in her community cringe.

Superstition was the essence of Anna Michel's beliefs, and many of her beliefs were conditioned or socialized into Anneliese as well. It was this mentality that made both women susceptible to moments of spiritual hysteria and certainly played a role in Anna's own neurosis and overbearing nature. Many of Anneliese's unreasonable fears, belief in being condemned, and delusions were rooted in Anna's behaviors, beliefs, and discussions regarding the spiritual realm.

Thea Heinz, a close friend and prominent member of the same parish attended by Anneliese and Anna, was the person who first suggested to Anna that her daughter may be possessed by demons. It is also known that Mrs. Heinz facilitated many of the clerical meetings with Jesuits throughout the area. This includes Father Alt and Father Renz. It appears that Thea held on to the same or very similar beliefs in curses, witchcraft, and demonic mayhem as those of Anna Michel. Anna adopted Thea's theory of demonic possession fervently and immediately went about the task of convincing her husband, Josef Michel, that demons were the culprits and not mental illness.

It was in 1971 that the book entitled *The Exorcist* was published. It was an immediate international success and significant increases in reported cases of suspected demonic possession were recorded as the book circulated throughout the world in many different languages. It is a case of social hysteria that has been studied extensively by cultural anthropologists and sociologists alike. "Possession fever," as it was labeled informally, grew exponentially when the book was made into a movie and released in Germany in 1974.

It was around this time (1971–73) when Anneliese Michel began to experience her first symptoms of what her priests and family believed to be demonic possession. The coincidence of the movie's release and everyone's frantic belief that the girl was possessed by demons is too great to ignore. The evidence discovered in the Anneliese Michel exorcism case definitely indicates that there was a sort of hysterical mental state of the priests, Mrs. Heinz, Anna Michel, Josef Michel, and Anneliese's siblings during the last months of Anneliese's life.

Father Alt, the cleric who described himself to be a psychic and telepath, reported during the 1977 investigation and the subsequent 1978 trial that he instantly became nauseated and was attacked by a demonic presence as soon as he saw letters written by Anna and Anneliese Michel.[26] He stated this in a letter to the bishop of Wurzburg, too.[27] Father Alt described swarms of flies and shadowy creatures scurrying about the place that quite literally could have come out of a scene from a movie.

---

26. Goodman, *Exorcism of Anneliese Michel*, 45.

27. Fr. Ernst Alt to Bishop Josef Stangl, September 30, 1974, quoted in Goodman.

2

Contributing Emotional and Developmental Issues

2.1 UNREASONABLE STANDARDS

IN VIEW OF THE pile of evidence collected by anthropologist Felicitas Goodman, and that available through court records, a picture of the Michel household can be drawn. It is what Anneliese revealed more openly to Dr. Lenner in the later years and what has been stated by her sisters in interviews and interrogations that indicate an exceptionally dysfunctional family unit. None of the children in the Michel family were permitted to do much of anything on their own, and literally all aspects of life were controlled.

Michel family life was very rigid and almost military in function and form. Both Anna Michel and Josef Michel had survived life in Nazi Germany, and Josef had suffered the trauma of war on the Eastern front. These life experiences profoundly shaped their personalities and the ways they interacted with their children.

In Anna's eyes, the family had to be absolutely perfect and conform to societal norms. There was no room to be different or do anything that would call attention to oneself or others in the family. Anna Michel, maiden name Fürge, grew up in an environment where half of her family marched off to war and never returned and half of her neighbors marched off to concentration camps and never returned. Individual thought and expression could result in a death sentence in her earlier years and a mental illness could result in a person being euthanized or sent off to some experimental camp run by Dr. Josef Mangele (the Angel of Death). She was raised in constant fear for her life.

Anna Michel was not vain or concerned only for her self; rather, she was fearful and concerned with her family's survival. Her concern for rumors in the community and within the church was indeed unreasonable but understandable for a person who had just survived one of the deadliest regimes on the planet and in history. She genuinely feared that bad things would be done to Anneliese and the rest of the family because of genetic or hereditary impurity. She feared being socially shunned because her children were not perfectly healthy and strong. These were all anxieties of recent history for Anna, and she had exceptional difficulty shedding herself of them. They were a deeply engrained part of her life and personality.

Josef Michel is a typical case of postwar emotional dysfunction. Most likely suffering from what would now be accepted as post-traumatic stress disorder (PTSD), Josef Michel lived a mostly quiet and withdrawn life. He loved his children and wife very much but showed little affection or emotion. In his wartime days, emotions could get a person killed, and so he learned to suppress them in order to survive. He would later enforce the suppression of emotions within the family.

Being raised by Anna and Josef Michel was difficult and near torturous in regards to emotional development. There existed a demand for the children to be utterly perfect in everything they did; there was a constant demand not to show individuality but to conform to archaic social rules. Expressions or emoting of anger and pain were not permitted and came with the harshest of penalties, and all of the children were expected to sacrifice themselves in order to satisfy the needs of their mother. There were no individual boundaries, privacy, or expression. Everything had to be suppressed, and the rest was oppressed in this household.

Religion was strictly taught and enforced upon every child. To question religion was a costly deed for anyone in the family unit. Additionally, it is suspected that items such as the rosary and other prayer relics were used as tools of manipulation. This provoked resentment and rejection of such things and of all elements of religious practice. Anneliese had particular expressions of anger, and her outbursts were often focused on the rosary and icons of the Virgin Mary. She saw these things as mechanisms of emotional oppression and was naturally angered by their use. Unfortunately, the possibly unstable Father Alt, her mother Anna Michel, and Thea Heinz would interpret this resentment for such icons as evidence of demonic possession.

2.2 ABSENCE OF EMOTIONAL SUPPORT

In the Michel family one thing was absolutely clear to every member. You were either the absolute best or an absolute failure in every endeavor. This rule most likely came from both parents, as both understood that in the realm of survival, coming in second means death.

For Josef Michel, the struggle between life and death was up close and personal during World War II. He would either kill or be killed by his opponent. He had to be superior, and he had to win or die. There were no recoveries from a mistake in such an environment as he experienced. Just surviving the harsh winter in Russia forced him to be fiercely competitive among his own comrades. He most likely watched many of his fellows die while thanking God it wasn't him.

For Anna Michel, coming in first meant the difference between eating or starving and having a roof over her head or sleeping in the streets. World War II was as horrible for German civilians as it was for their soldiers. Anna Michel developed a compulsion to be the best, and being the best was just simply the norm for those who survive. She also had a deep-seated tendency to avoid anything that drew attention to her or the family as a result of living under the terror of the Nazi regime for so much of her life.

For the children of Anna and Josef Michel, life seems to have been near impossible. They were expected to be the best at all endeavors without exception. If they failed or ranked second place at something, they were chastised, ridiculed, and berated by their parents—more by their mother than their father, but the unreasonable demand for perfection was rooted in both parents. If they came in first or had the highest grade, they were most likely not rendered congratulations or any form of positive reinforcement. This was the standard, and there was nothing exceptional for merely meeting the standard. So, success was never recognized with joy or celebration—it was simply expected.

Anneliese Michel grew up in an emotional vacuum. There was no consolation for sadness or loss and no encouragement to achieve in the instance of failure or perceived failure. A person who wasn't perfect was called a loser, viewed as a worthless being, or became an embarrassment to her parents. A person who could not control her emotions of sadness or anger was considered weak and treated as if worthless baggage.

Affection was withdrawn and used as a weapon or manipulation tool against those children, including Anneliese, who failed to live up to parental expectations. These conditions shaped Anneliese's self-image and self-esteem. This is where she developed the perception that she was worthless, evil, and would never accomplish anything that would make her parents happy. The self-image of being an evil person would give rise to her later establishment of the Satan personality.

2.3 SIGNIFICANT LIFE STRESSORS

If a chart is drawn to show stress levels throughout the lifespan of Anneliese Michel, her approximate level of coping, the frequency of seizures, and the frequency of psychotic episodes, an immediate correlation is observed. As the stress level exceeds Anneliese's ability to cope, the frequency and intensity of her seizures and hallucinatory experiences rise. The longer the stress level endures, the worse and more permanent the conditions become.

For Anneliese, significant life stress came every time a major written examination approached in school. She was not worried about simply passing these examinations but scoring perfectly on them. She was under intense personal and parental pressure to achieve the statistically unachievable. This stress quickly ran beyond the maximum level with which she could cope, and the seizures returned in frequent and intense measure. These attacks were accompanied by temporary moments of psychosis as healthy coping broke down.

A second area of severe stress for Anneliese was in living conditions. In reviewing her symptom history, it is clearly seen that moving away from what she was comfortable with created intense stress as she struggled to adapt to new social environments and personalities. Anneliese's maternally over-controlled life left her with an underdeveloped ability to adapt to new social environments. The stress of moving into the clinic as a child brought on epileptic episodes and the beginning of her psychotic experiences, and her moving out into the dormitories while attending college sparked the same thing except with more intensity.

A third consideration is in the longevity of excessive stress levels in Anneliese's life. Stressors that lasted for longer terms before falling below her coping level seemed to allow for the permanent development of worsened psychosis. It was as if each period of uncontrollable stress created permanent chemical changes inside her brain that allowed for the worsening and eventual deterioration of her mental and medical state.

But, because the priests were primarily blinded by demonic hysteria, or possession fever, and had little training in the areas of sociology and psychology, these elements of her life were either ignored or completely unknown to them. They were certainly smart enough to know better than to move forward with an exorcism with so few facts in hand, though. For modern exorcists, emotional development and a comparative of stress and behavior is a requirement in the investigation and evaluation of suspected demonic possession. The key here is that demons are rather constant while mental illness usually has a triggering mechanism and an oscillatory charted pattern that correlates with stress levels and stressor types.

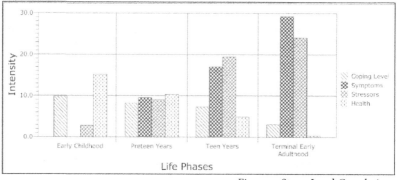

Figure 1. Stress Level Correlation

2.4 RELATIONSHIPS WITH PARENTS

Dr. Lenner, Anneliese's therapist, reported to investigators in 1977 that the young girl suffered from a classic case of neurosis rooted in a father who didn't understand her and a mother for whom she had great hatred.[1] The assessment seems to generally sum up the relationship Anneliese had with her parents. It seems to illustrate her feelings that resulted from

1. Goodman, *Exorcism of Anneliese Michel*, 53.

an overly controlling and demanding mother and a father that she was unable to turn to for emotional support.

Anneliese's hatred for her mother seems to fit the classic resentment felt by a child who is in a one-sided relationship with a parent. She most likely was required to sacrifice her feelings, dignity, and independence constantly in order to meet her mother's demands and needs. Very little positive affection was rendered to her by her mother in return. She probably held great resentment for her mother's behavior and regard toward her.

Josef Michel was a presence in her life and development but was not much of a nurturer or consoler for Anneliese. As a result, she had no means of relieving herself of the anxiety and frustration that came from her emotionally distressing relationship with her mother. It is clear that Anneliese loved her father very much but was unable to emotionally connect with him, and thus she was left with few places to turn for emotional support.

Her mother's use of religion as a tool to oppress individuality and emotion, use of affection withdrawal to manipulate and control, and harsh and cruel criticism undoubtedly built up a huge mass of anger and rage inside Anneliese toward her mother. She may have even entertained thoughts of killing or physically harming her mother in anger. Such thoughts would have been quite scary to Anneliese, and she would have also felt guilty for even having such a thought.

Such guilt would certainly explain how her later manifestation of the Cain personality came to be. After all, Cain murdered his brother and then wore the mark of guilt for the rest of his life. Her desire and need to express and relieve inner rage explains the manifestation of the Hitler personality. In developing into an adult, Anneliese would have a natural desire to break away from her mother and become an independent individual. She may have consequently experienced inner conflict as she desired individuality but was taught conformity and codependence. There would certainly be room for the development of the Judas personality also, because he turned away and rejected Christ as she wanted to turn and break away from her mother.

2.5 RELATIONSHIPS WITH SIBLINGS

Anneliese appears to have had a very close relationship with her sisters. This was especially so for Gertrud and Roswitha Michel. Her diary reflects a genuine loneliness when she was separated from her sisters. There is evidence that her sisters Gertrud, Barbara, and Roswitha offered as much emotional and physical support as they could to Anneliese as she went through those nightmarish ordeals.

Additionally, the moving out of the home by both Barbara and Gertrud Michel generated life stress levels that, in combination with other stressors, triggered emotional and epileptic problems for Anneliese. She was very sensitive to even the slightest change in her life routines.

No evidence has been discovered that shows any sort of sibling rivalry or resentments relative to parental favoritism. They seem to have all clung to each other as they shared in their mother's oppressiveness and their father's supportive vacancy. Anneliese's diary does not reveal any bad feelings or resentments for her sisters at all. Instead, there was great love for them, and she missed them when they were not present. A graphic depiction of the Michel family would show that the sisters were all close, their mother a distant and static relation and their father distant from them but opposite of their mother. Some call this a family grouping graph.

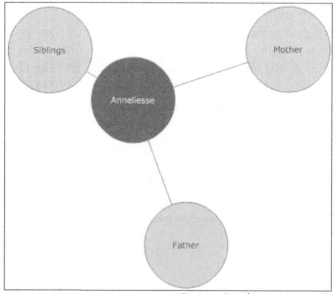

Figure 2. Family grouping graph

2.6 CLERICAL AND RELIGIOUS RELATIONSHIPS

Anneliese had a well-engrained and deep Roman Catholic faith. She was well known for her devotion to the church and was even described by classmates as a sort of "religion nut." She looked upon members of the priesthood as if they were of some special and magical order. The reverence she had for priests, nuns, and saintly characters made her exceptionally obedient and accepting of literally anything they said.

A person like Father Ernst Alt, described by psychologists as being an abnormal personality with reported experiences that qualified as schizophrenic psychosis, wielded unusual influence over young Anneliese. If any priest told her that she was being tormented by demons or even possessed by them, she would accept it without question or doubt of any kind. Her mental state enhanced this vulnerability to suggestion by Father Alt.

To a degree, Anneliese was correct in saying that she was under the influence of someone else. Her hallucinations and delusions manifested through and from her but could have been molded and manipulated by Father Alt. There was no doubting that Ernst Alt was a fervent reader of books by writers such as William Blatty (*The Exorcist*) and Malachi Martin (*Hostage to the Devil*) and had seen the 1973 movie *The Exorcist*. In his own possibly delusional state, he went forth to conquer the Prince of Darkness with stories and images of demonic warfare dancing through his head.

In regards to what may have chiefly motivated Father Alt to insist on an exorcism performance, even when other priests observed no possession-related symptoms, there are two possibilities. In fact, both factors may have been at play in this catastrophic incident. First, Father Alt may have genuinely believed that the girl was possessed and wanted to be a modern day Knight Templar wielding his sword against evil to save a fair maiden. The other motivational possibility is far less glamorous and even sinister in nature. Father Alt may have been desirous of the same level of fame and fortune achieved by the likes William Blatty and Malachi Martin. He may indeed have had plans to write a book like *Der Dämon von Klingenberg* (The Demon from Klingenburg) or something along those lines.

For Father Renz, the assistant exorcist and codefendant in this case, things were considerably different. He also underwent a psychological evaluation by the same psychiatrists who examined Father Alt. However, they did not note anything that indicated instability in the mental abilities or health of Father Renz. They did note that he was a bit indecisive and unclear in regards to the sole topic of exorcism and suggested that it may have been due to a calcification in his brain. This anomaly was detected during a CT scan and was deemed as not life threatening.

By all accounts, Father Renz was an intelligent person who was simply gullible to anything suggested by Father Alt. He did see Father Alt as being the most authoritative person on the subjects of demonology and exorcism. Others have expressed a belief that Father Renz did not see himself as knowing enough about the subject to question the actions and inactions of Father Alt. Regardless, he did watch the girl literally waste away without seeking or rendering aid.

It is entirely possible that Father Renz had been preconditioned by conversations with Father Alt and was also in a form of religious hysteria when he arrived at the Michel home. Father Renz arrived the day before the first exorcism and noted that had he not been told of the possession beforehand he would not have believed the girl was suffering from demonic possession.[2] In addition to the suspected preconditioning by Father Alt, Father Renz had read the books entitled *Exorcism Today* and *Exorcism according to the Rituale Romanum* by Father Rodewyk, a well-known German expert on possession and exorcism.

2.7 CLOSE FRIENDS

A normal consequence to Anneliese Michel's mental deterioration and the isolation imposed by her mother was the lack of close friends. Anneliese did have one friend with whom she grew up and even went to college. This was Maria Burdich, and although they did spend time together frequently, Anneliese was unable to establish enough interest in her friend to listen to Anneliese's experiences and relational issues with her mother.

Other than Maria, Anneliese did manage to fall in love and develop a deep emotionally and sexually intimate relationship with a young man named Peter while attending college. He was very close to her and did not leave her side throughout all of her difficulties. It was definitely a relationship that, under less strenuous and tragic circumstances, could

---

2. Goodman, *Exorcism of Anneliese Michel*, 93.

have led to a good and strong marriage between the two. Although he did not fully understand Anneliese's behavioral issues, he remained optimistic that there would one day be a cure for her. There is insufficient evidence to indicate that Peter actually believed that Anneliese was possessed or being manipulated by demons or Satan.

Anneliese Michel, as with almost all other schizophrenics, suffered from an inability to interact well with others. The more unknown to her they were, the more uncomfortable she became. Even when literally forced to interact with a person or group of people, Anneliese would remain silent and say very little if anything at all. Her boyfriend, Peter, tried many times to introduce her to his rather large circle of friends, but often she would refuse to go and meet them or avoid directly engaging them when she was persuaded to meet and mingle.

PART 2

Demonic Possession

Always behind what we imagine are our best deeds stands the
devil, patting us paternally on the shoulder and whispering,
"Well done!"

—Carl G. Jung, *A Psychological View of Conscience*

3

Defining Possession

3.1 CATHOLIC DEFINITIONS

A DEBATE HAS BEEN raging between clergy, theologians, and lay ministers within the Roman church regarding the physical existence of Satan and his demons. On one side of the fence are those who believe that Satan has both a physical and spiritual existence and can therefore do as he pleases in either realm—that of the flesh and that of the spirit. On the other side of the debate stand those who believe that Satan was never given a physical form or an ability to assume one by God. These biblical scholars assert that Satan and his many demons are incapable of having independent physical forms on earth and exist solely in a formless spirit.

These two schools of thought have a profound effect on how possession is viewed, determined, and rationalized within the Roman Catholic Church. Determining which perspective is correct really depends on what level of credence is given by the observer. The evidence is strong in both camps. However, possession seems more easily accepted and logically explained from the perspective of Satan's solely spiritual existence.

Nobody has credibly reported seeing and touching Satan. There are no documented cases of a demonic entity in physical or flesh form. Even those who claim to have been physically attacked by demons do not see the attacker but feel only the damage done by the attack. Such testimony would serve to support the solely spiritual existence more than a physical existence.

Generally, demonic possession is defined as the entering into and controlling of a human body by Satan or other demonic entity. Both schools of thought regarding Satan's existence agree that this is exactly what demonic possession is. But, for those who believe in a physical form of Satanic existence, possession is seen as an event of exceptional rarity. Their position on the matter is that if Satan and his demons have physical bodies of their own, what need have they of a weaker human body? It is indeed a sound argument. For the advocates of a purely spiritual form of satanic existence, the condition of possession is a frequent event. These individuals see possession as the only means for Satan and his demons to enter into the earthly realm in a physical form.

In contemporary times, the predominant theory seems to lean toward a solely spiritual existence of satanic entities with an ability to manipulate things physically. Thus, they cannot be touched, seen, heard, or smelled in the physical sense. This occurs only through spiritual influences that allow targeted people to see, hear, smell, and be touched by them. In this perspective, demonic possession is entirely possible and for some scholars very frequent. However, the church and most of its clergy take into account the strategic and tactical significance of a demonic possession.

It is important to keep in mind that the Vatican's official stance is that Satan does have a physical form of his own. This declaration hasn't reduced objection and opposing views on the subject within the ranks of the clergy or among Catholic theologians, though. The debate certainly didn't end with the official position statement but simply went underground.

Never should any person assume that Satan and his subordinate demons lack intellect and keen reasoning skills. Such would be a fatal mistake, as demons are indeed among the most intelligent and cunning creatures in existence. Being intelligent creatures, demons will not expend energy on anything that fails to produce desired results at minimal cost. Thus, possession will only be executed where there is great gain for the demonic entity (or entities) involved.

To possess a human body, the demon makes a victim of the possessed and thus any outcry for help will be immediately reacted to by God and the angels of heaven. Satan and his demons have very little chance of surviving a direct tactical engagement with angelic forces. It is tactically unsound to seize someone for the sole purpose of dooking it out with priests and angels. There is too much energy, too much risk, and insufficient gain for the demonic entity. However, there are certainly strategic advantages for demonic possession.

What could be gained strategically by Satan through demonic influence or possession? If such were to be executed against a wealthy and politically influential person, then much could be gained. If Lucifer were to invade a body or make a deal with a person (which is far more preferable as the person also becomes a willing warrior against God and Christ) who was charismatic, influential in many matters of finance and state, and wielding great power over a large mass of people, then many people could be led away from God and convinced to willfully commit heinous acts of sin against others and in defiance of the Lord, our God.

An example of this would be Adolf Hitler, a person who was already evil and easily brought into Satan's plan to capture the souls of not hundreds but of millions while wreaking death and destruction upon God's chosen people, the Jews. Hitler's speeches entranced millions who then willfully turned away from God, acted to offend God, destroyed God's temples, and violated all of the Ten Commandments. These people willfully followed Hitler into condemnation for eternity. This was a strategic success for Lucifer as he was able to gather in millions of German SS, Nazi members, gestapo, and others who were directly responsible for the destruction and death wrought upon the earth. Those who put them in power carry much burden and responsibility, too.

This is where possession and demonic influence can be of great advantage to the diabolical elements of the universe. It is not worth the energy or time of a demon to inhabit the body of a person who wields no power or stands to inherit no power in the future. However, there is great danger of demonic activity in regards to an opportunity to use one body to influence millions of other souls.

The argument of whether or not the devil has both a physical and spiritual form doesn't appear to be as prevalent throughout the Orthodox churches as is the case within the Roman Church. The general consensus is that Satan does indeed have a physical body and is indeed capable of engaging humans in physical and spiritual realms. In this line of thinking, many dismiss the concept of possession by demons. They argue that there is no reason to occupy a human body when they have their own.

In discussing the matter of strategic influence or possession by demons, many Orthodox priests have expressed agreement that where one could lead many into damnation the likelihood that possession or influence would occur is great.

In North America there are several other smaller Roman offshoot churches. These churches retain much of the doctrines and processes of the traditional Roman Catholic Church but adopt less conservative applications and interpretations of them. Churches such as the Old Catholic Church, American Catholic Church, Polish Reformed Catholic Church, Reformed Catholic Church, and Ecumenical Catholic Church consider themselves Catholic and celebrate the Mass and Communion in the same way. Differences include positions on birth control, the marriage of priests, and even the acceptance of homosexuals as clergy.

For the conservative Reformed Catholic Church of North America (not to be confused with the very liberal American Catholic Church), the position that Satan is primarily a spiritual entity has been adopted. Satan and his demons are seen as very rarely invading and controlling the bodies of humans and only for purposes that result in great gain for the dark forces against God. Thus, possession occurs but not frequently or arbitrarily. For these Catholics, determining possession requires the meeting or satisfying of a very strict list of criteria. The extent and thoroughness of investigation and the considerations applied for safety and health go far beyond those of the Roman Catholic Church's doctrine.

3.2 PROTESTANT CHRISTIAN DEFINITIONS

There are an overwhelming number of Protestant churches in North America alone. And, there is no real general consensus as to what demonic possession is and what should be done to remedy the condition. Detailing the definitive perspectives of each church would be too voluminous to be of any good in this book. So, I have chosen the one perspective on the topic that comes up most frequently in conversations with various church leaders across the United States and other nations. The reader is advised that there are other perspectives held by various Protestant faiths, some of which directly conflict with the one presented in this book.

The most common perspective encountered throughout my research for this book was that the devil existed in both spiritual and physical form. He is seen as operating simultaneously in both realms with his many subordinate demons. Many Protestant leaders believe that Satan and his demons are ever present and working hard to tempt humanity away from God and into sin. They see him more as an entity that negatively influences humanity rather than one to take over a person's body.

Repeatedly, we see preachers talk about Satan and his minions whispering things into the ears of the faithful and helping them to rationalize sin so as to be trapped into condemnation. Very seldom is it heard that Satan enters the body of a person and completely takes them over. Even in evangelical deliverance services demons are seen as being inside the body but acting only as tempters and sinful urges rather than absolute physical controllers.

Demonic possession and influence thus is seen in a vastly different light by Protestants, compared to Catholics. As a result, the process of casting out demons is different as well. In fact, few Protestant practitioners call the ritual *exorcism*. Instead, they prefer to call their process a *deliverance service*. The concept behind these rituals is to literally deliver the afflicted person away from the influence of demonic forces so as to enable him or her to live once again in the grace of God.

For most Protestant faiths, Satan and his demons regularly enter and harass humans. But, they manifest themselves in a way that differs from what is believed by Catholics. In prevailing Protestant concepts, demons enter the body and act as urges or voices of temptation that cause the individual to willfully sin or to reject God entirely. They also assert the belief that Satan enters those who, through their deeds and thoughts, have invited evil into their lives and bodies. Thus, possession is a consequence of sin, and the possessed is not an innocent person but worthy of salvation.

The devil is seen as a great tempter and deceiver whose primary purpose is to cause a person to lose his or her relationship with God as the devil has lost his own relationship with God. Lucifer's jealousy of humanity and resentment of God's love for humanity is immense. Therefore, he and his demons strive to cause the fall of humanity and cause pain in God. The rationalizations of sin and the liberalization of biblical interpretation and church tradition are his tools to lead people away from God's grace and the salvation of Jesus Christ.

Whether one is delivering a person away from demonic forces or exorcising demonic forces out of the person, the goal, in both sectors of Christendom, remains the same. The desire is to separate a person from the demonic so as to save humanity from suffering and condemnation. Indeed, the perspectives and approaches differ while the outcome and goal is identical throughout Christendom.

4

Christian Criteria for Determining Possession

4.1 ROMAN RITUAL

NO ONE IS CERTAIN as to when an official ritual for the expulsion of demons from the human body was first created or used by the Roman Catholic Church. However, there are Old Testament references to demonic expulsions, with enhancements being seen in the New Testament.[1] It is known that exorcism actually became an incorporated element of the baptismal ritual around 200 AD.[2] The earliest exorcism ritual publications available for review date to the Middle Ages.

The earlier official documents regarding the process of exorcism included a great many references to superstitions and even magical incantations that the modern Vatican rejects.[3] Many revisions have taken place over the years, with the version seen in the *Roman Ritual* series originally published in 1952 and republished in 2007. The Roman exorcism rite is a continuously morphing spiritual activity, and will, someday, incorporate medical science and psychology in a more productive, safer, and healthier manner. But, at present the Roman rite simply advises the

---

1. Hagen, *Die Lehre der Heiligen Schrift uber den Teufel*, 55:368, cited in Weller, trans., *Roman Ritual*, 2:165.

2. Weller, *Roman Ritual*, 2:165.

3. Weller, *Roman Ritual*, 2:166.

priest to be sure that no mental or physical illness is the culprit rather than demonic forces.

One of the first things one reads in the exorcism rite[4] is "not to believe too readily that a person is possessed by an evil spirit, but to ascertain the signs by which a person possessed can be distinguished from one who is suffering from melancholy or some other illness."[5] This is a key point and an important step in the investigation of suspected possession. It requires the priest to approach his evaluation of the afflicted person with objectivity and a certain level of skepticism.

Through an objective and scientifically skeptical approach, the evaluator is permitted to see people, places, and events as they really are rather than how his emotions would otherwise interpret them to be. The evidence must prove beyond all reason and earthly explanation that the person is possessed by a demonic spirit. If anything less than this standard is applied, then there is a great risk of misidentifying the ailment or condition. The early and contemporary church sees this very important approach perspective and literally requires it.

There is another concern regarding objective and strict comparative study of the criteria for possession and the actual condition of the afflicted person. Few members of the clergy like to admit that reputation and credibility both make and break churches. There is no greater defeat for Christ and no greater victory for Satan than for a church to lose its credibility and to become subject to justified ridicule. Such a situation could lead many to reject Christ and turn away from God and into the fiery ovens of hell. Therefore, it is of great importance to be absolutely sure that what is being dealt with is of demonic origin before snapping to conclusions.

The Roman ritual for exorcism does mandate that an objective and thorough investigation of the suspected possession victim be conducted. But, it focuses more on fitting the evidence with the criteria rather than first following a process of medical and scientific elimination. This is seen in the statement, "to ascertain those signs by which a person possessed can be distinguished from one who is suffering from melancholy or some other illness."[6] This has led to the development of narrow-mindedness in the investigating priests. To look only at those elements

4. Weller, *Roman Ritual*, 2:159.
5. Weller, *Roman Ritual*, 2:167, 169.
6. Weller, *Roman Ritual*, 2:166.

that fit the criteria while ignoring evidence of some medical or mental illness defeats objectivism and undermines any effort at thoroughness in the investigation.

What exactly are the criteria listed in the exorcism rite for determining whether a person is ill, a fraud, or truly possessed by demonic forces? According to paragraph 3 of the document entitled *The Exorcism of the Possessed*, there are four determining elements. These possession indicators are an ability to speak and understand languages unknown to the afflicted person, an ability to tell of unknown or future events, a display of powers that go well beyond the natural human condition, and other indications that cumulatively indicate demonic possession. Every priest, minister, exorcist, and scholar agrees that this list is both too short and entirely too vague.

The very natures of the listed indicators infer a requirement to conduct a thorough investigation in regard to the afflicted person. This is especially so for his or her personal history. How else is one to know that the person is speaking in a language that is completely unknown to him or her? Without being completely familiar with the individual's medical, mental, and historical records the priest is not in a position to know if the individual is displaying strength or skills that go beyond his or her normal human condition. Granted, situations where the afflicted person hovers above the ground will certainly satisfy the criterion for powers beyond the normal human state.

4.2 BEYOND THE ROMAN RITE

Aside from the *Roman Ritual* there really are no theological documents, especially within Protestant circles, that attempt to establish standard criteria for determining the presence or actual condition of demonic possession. Most exorcists are left with having to acquire direct experience in the school of trial and error. That approach is exceptionally dangerous for everyone involved. But, there are a plethora of experienced demonological writers and experts, with various theological and clerical credentials, who have indicated what they would interpret as demonic.

Criteria, therefore, must be collected and assessed from a seemingly endless pile of resource books and papers on the topic of demons, demonic possession, and exorcism. It is a very long and laborious process that is complicated by conflicting theories and opposing views. The

absence of a Christian-wide acceptable list of standard demonic possession signs and symptoms has been and remains a major contributing
factor to the misclassification of demonic possession.

In the Klingenberg case, described in part 1 of this book, it is absolutely clear that the priests had no idea as to what was meant by the
criteria listed in the *Roman Ritual* and those written by leading Catholic
demonologists and exorcists of the time. Many of the written works
on the subject were unavailable to them, too. In more recent times, a
Romanian nun, who was diagnosed with schizophrenia, was killed during an exorcism when she was denied food and water by the Orthodox
exorcist and attending nuns. This, too, was due to not completely understanding the true signs and symptoms of demonic possession.

4.3 INVESTIGATING DEMONIC POSSESSION

Oddly, the *Roman Ritual* is absent of a detailed and standardized method
for investigating, collecting evidence, and documenting facts in cases of
suspected diabolic possession. Throughout the church's history, investigation has consisted of observations that may or may not be contempo-
raneous in documentation. Because there was no actual procedure for
investigation, many facts were lost, forgotten, or overlooked entirely. It is
like asking a florist to investigate a homicide or a construction worker to
excavate a significant archaeological site. The results are disastrous and
many times dangerous.

Many exorcists, priestly and otherwise, jot down notes, but the gen-
eration of formal reports and documentation hardly ever takes place.
Exorcists explain that things happen too quickly or that spiritual matters are subject to what they feel. Some state that they fear use of the
documents against them in court. Indeed, there are very few items of
formal documentation on events and activities of the investigator that
shed light on how and upon what the exorcist made the determination
of demonic possession.

For the most part, reports are written in letter form that expresses
an accumulation of evidence indicative of possession. Almost always
these reports leave out facts that would otherwise indicate an illness
rather than possession. Never are copies of health records, physicals,
mental evaluations, or interviews with key people included in a report.

The letter goes to the bishop, who has not even seen the afflicted person, for third-party supervisor review and approval for the exorcism rite.

Additionally, the exorcism rite renders no direction or requirement to perform mental evaluations, medical physicals, and other crucial information gathering activities. This is mainly due to the fact that the rite hasn't undergone a serious revision since the late 1960s, following the Vatican II council. The requirement is for the priest to gather and report only the evidence that distinguishes the person's affliction from illness of the mind or body. This has left room for incomplete and haphazard investigation, biased reporting to superiors, loss in objectivity, and erroneous determination of demonic possession.

Over many centuries the scientific community and the religious community have drifted apart. Neither sees the other as an important element to the investigation and determination of demonic possession. But, in fact they are very important to one another and to the safety and well-being of the person experiencing possession or illness. Psychologists, sociologists, anthropologists, and priests all agree that people do experience what is often described as demonic possession. Whether it is merely an experience or a live demonic event is irrelevant in regard to what the subject believes to be a very real happening.

In recent times, members of the clergy, especially within the Reformed Catholic Church of North America, have begun to see scientists not as blasphemers but as discoverers and explorers. Scientists didn't invent physics; they discovered it. Scientists didn't invent the biological mechanisms of the living cell; they discovered them. Even in space, they are discoverers of God's universe and of God's laws. They use these laws, once discovered, to do both good and bad throughout the world.

At the same time, members of the medical establishment have begun to realize that faith is a huge enhancement to the healing process. Faith gives hope and optimism, which reduces stress and allows the body to fight disease or mend injuries more easily. Psychologists have also realized that faith and belief in God have a profound effect on the human mental condition. Cultural anthropologists have discovered that demonic possession is experienced by human beings in almost every world culture.

In the investigation of suspected demonic possession, it is important for the investigating cleric to include elements of medical and mental health science. It is also beneficial to have a basic sociological understanding of the subject's social environment. People who professionally study human behavior are perfect assistants to priests who engage in the proper process of eliminating all possible earthly ailments and probabilities before concluding with a determination of demonic possession.

It is most unfortunate that the Roman Catholic Church does not require mental and medical specialists in the process of investigating suspected possession. Although some bishops have individually required the involvement of medical and mental health professionals, there is no regulatory requirement for it. The results over the years have been mentally and physically damaging exorcisms and costly embarrassment for the Church of Rome and other Catholic churches.

In my many research interviews conducted with clergymen and -women of various Protestant faiths, it has been observed that superstition exists at a nearly medieval level. This observation was not made of Lutheran, Presbyterian, and Episcopal clergy, but certainly there was substantial reliance and proliferation of superstitious ideas regarding demonic topics throughout Protestant Christendom. These superstitious positions were indeed held by the Orthodox and Roman Catholic churches in the 1300s but have since been rejected in their entirety. The likelihood of misdiagnosed demonic possession is tremendously higher among and within the various Protestant faiths than by Roman or related Catholic churches.

For many Protestant exorcists, medical history and mental condition seem to be of the lowest importance. These investigators call in alleged psychics and spiritual mediums to determine the presence of dark forces in or near a person. There are no statements, comparative studies, or collections of tangible evidence made. The process of elimination in investigation is scarcely even known by these investigators and third-party review with supervisory level authorization is nonexistent. A Protestant investigation of suspected demonic activity would be laughable if the potential consequences weren't so severe.

4.4 REPORTING FINDINGS AND RECOMMENDATIONS

As can be seen in the Klingenberg case, there is absolutely no standard Roman Catholic format or requirement in reporting on suspected cases of possession and on the activities of exorcism ritual. The bishop of Wurzburg rendered approval for an exorcism based on incomplete and biased investigation with absolutely no way of knowing otherwise. Bishop Stangl's error was in rendering an approval on something he knew little about. The result was a true and avoidable tragedy. He most certainly should have demanded more supportive evidence and the elimination of all earthly conditions or ailments.

For the most part, a priest who investigates a suspected exorcism writes a letter that outlines his findings and conclusions. This is all that the supervising bishop sees or knows of the case, and the likelihood of error on the part of the bishop is incredibly and dangerously high. The bishop literally has no way of knowing if all of the facts are being considered or if they are being overlooked in order to manipulate perceptions. Additionally, he has no access to the raw data related to the case in order to evaluate the priest's conclusions in the matter.

It is far worse among the Protestant faiths, as there are no written rules whatsoever on the matter. Some churches do have formal regulations, but these are clearly pointed at covering the church from any legal liability that may result from an exorcism or deliverance service. A good example of this is on the wordplay used by many churches in implementing the term *deliverance* rather than *exorcism*. There are no requirements to seek advice or approval from bishops or other supervisory officials, and thus reporting standards are completely thrown out the window.

Ministers and lay exorcists are left to perform these activities entirely on their own. The preacher must investigate a case of suspected demonic activity, determine if actual demoniacal presence and influence is occurring, and then perform the deliverance or exorcism alone. Being as human as any other person, the minister is subject to human error caused by misinterpretation, fatigue, subject matter ignorance, superstition, and personal bias. There are no checks and balances integrated into the process at all. Needless to say, this constitutes a formula for disaster.

5

The Rite of Exorcism

5.1 PREPARATORY ACTIVITIES

PIETY AND HUMILITY ARE the two most important prerequisites for a priest, according to the *Roman Ritual*.[1] The selected priest must be of exceptional religious wisdom and be a very pious and humble servant of God. He must be advanced in years so as to be of the highest level of life experience within the church and of worldly matters. Such persons make the best choices for demonic warfare. But, there is more to this requirement than just wisdom and experience.

In the exorcism of Anneliese Michel we see that a younger priest of questionable intentions and mental stability is at the root of the disaster that occurred in Klingenberg. A person in more advanced years would have more time to develop and display the signs and symptoms in behavior that is indicative of a less stable personality. Thus, such a person would most certainly not have been considered for or authorized to perform an exorcism. Additionally, a person with more years experience would be in a better position to recognize insanity over demoniacal activity in the subject.

Delving further into the Roman exorcism rite, there is a requirement that the selected priest "be immune to any striving for human aggrandizement . . . and be revered not alone for his office but for his moral

---

1. Weller, *Roman Ritual*, 2:169.

qualities."[2] In other words, the exorcist must not be seeking fame or fortune in his efforts to remove demons from a suffering Christian. Yet, this is something we see quite often from priests and ministers around the world who have profited greatly from high-dollar lectures and books following their alleged exploits as exorcists. It is essential that the priest have a genuine desire to help another suffering human being and that he not have any other profit or fame-gaining intentions in mind.

There is no doubting that by 1975 Father Ernst Alt was quite familiar with the written works of William Blatty (*The Exorcist*) and Malachi Martin (*Hostage to the Devil* and other works). These authors, along with numerous others who wrote theses and articles on exorcism, acquired instant recognition and fame. Father Alt's quite biased letters to Bishop Stangl in Wurzburg seem to evidence a desire to acquire a bit of fame for himself. Where every other priest, including experienced exorcists, declined to participate in the Anneliese Michel exorcism, Father Alt continued anyway. It is a clear possibility, in reviewing the evidence collected for the 1978 criminal trial, that Father Ernst Alt was determined to get an exorcism case under his belt that he could also write books about and conduct lectures on. Why else would he be so diligent to record the actual exorcism sessions but none of the evidence that supported or refuted a determination of demonic possession?

Before the priest or approved lay minister even arrives at the location of the allegedly possessed, he must first go into deep prayer for strength and the presence of Christ, God, and all the angels in heaven.[3] Additionally, he should go to confession and receive absolution.[4] It is not the power of the priest alone but that of God Almighty who dismisses evil spirits and things from the realm of the living world and beyond. The priest or lay minister should take care to recognize this and pray for the assistance and support of God and the many angels. In addition, the *Roman Ritual* states that the exorcist himself should be free of sin, having been absolved of his transgressions through confession and the act of contrition.

It was revealed by Father Arnold Renz, the assisting exorcist in the Klingenberg case, during the 1978 criminal trial that prayer, fasting, and study of the subject was performed. There is no doubting that Father

2. Weller, *Roman Ritual*, 2:169.
3. Weller, *Roman Ritual*, 2:167.
4. Weller, *Roman Ritual*, 2:175.

Renz was indeed a very pious man and a person of admirable integrity. However, there is no evidence whatsoever that Father Alt performed these required actions himself. It is indeed doubtful that he did any of these prerequisite things in view of how many elements of the *Roman Ritual* he ignored in his alleged investigation of Anneliese's suspected demonic possession.

The Roman rite requires several things of the person chosen to perform an exorcism: One is that the priest be of advanced years and experience, while the second is that he be humble, genuinely caring, and nondesirous of fame and fortune at the expense of people in suffering. He must be cleansed of all inequities through confession, contrition, and absolution, too. Though the Roman Church has long required this, clergymen within and outside of the church have continually ignored it and performed erroneous and botched exorcisms for the sole purpose of writing and lecturing about it. Their desire to reach the fame and fortune of William Blatty has driven them to perform exorcisms where none is needed and to create issues and incidents of incredible detriment and embarrassment to the church.

5.2 EXECUTING THE EXORCISM RITE

The actual Roman exorcism ritual consists of eleven prayers and seventeen biblical text readings. It lasts only about twenty to twenty-five minutes. But, it is generally believed that a single performance of the exorcism ritual, as proscribed by the *Rituale Romanum*, must be repeated numerous times in order for the demon(s) to be truly and completely removed from the seized subject. This means that a single exorcism session can last anywhere from a couple of hours to twelve hours. And, there can be numerous sessions that last for weeks or even months. There is no set time on how long it takes to remove a demon or numerous demons, as many cases appear to have shown.

The subject can be taken to a church or other prepared place for the exorcism; however, it is preferred that it be a church.[5] Many have misunderstood this element of the ritual to mean that the possessed person should be taken into the sanctuary for the performance of the exorcism. This is not what is meant; rather, the exorcism should be performed in

---

5. Weller, *Roman Ritual*, 2:171.

a room of the church away from the sanctuary while remaining on holy and controlled grounds. The principle is that holy grounds make for weakened demons.

Interestingly, the Roman ritual does state that if the subject is mentally or medically incapable of being taken to a church then the exorcism should be performed in a home or other place. In regards to medical ailments or conditions, one can easily understand and agree with the conducting of exorcism rituals in the subject's home or other more suitable place. But, it mentions mental illness in this statement. Why it includes mental illness when the possibility of mental illness should be eliminated prior to concluding the presence or activities of demonic entities is unclear. Perhaps there is some unknown and unwritten rule regarding this that can't be easily explored at this time. Perhaps this was what rendered sufficient excuse to Fathers Alt and Renz to ignore clear symptoms of mental illness in Ms. Anneliese Michel and continue with the exorcism even when they could see that her health was becoming critical.

The approach to conducting a deliverance service depends on which denomination is involved. The absence of a standardized and written ritual or procedure has become a common theme among the hundreds of Protestant denominations and their many more subfactions. In some cases, there are significant differences between individual ministers serving under the same denomination. But, generally each minister is on his or her own to design and perform a deliverance service.

Most commonly, a deliverance service is much like a regular Sunday service but with a limited number of people. Usually, the service is conducted at the afflicted person's home or other suitable area other than the church building or grounds. In observing deliverances, one cannot help but notice how much more dramatic and fevered the atmosphere is in comparison to the ritual of exorcism performed by Catholics. The minister often reads Scripture and makes demands that the demon(s) depart the victim. Prayers and actions are made on the fly, and therefore nothing is repeated exactly from one moment to another. Several biblical sections may be reread as the hours tick by, but there is no real end for a repeating session to follow.

Some ministers will write out what prayers they will say and what texts will be read in a deliverance service. In these cases, there exists a clearly organized approach to casting out demons. These situations will

show a repeated pattern over hours of prayer and demonic confrontation. However, these approaches are created on a case-by-case basis
and often overlook or omit crucial items or perspectives in confronting
demons while maintaining a healthy and safe physical and emotional
environment for all people involved in the service.

Another difference between Catholic and Protestant ritual approaches to cases of demonic possession or molestation is the existence
of differing levels of services within the Roman Church, and other
Catholic churches, that simply do not exist within the many Protestant
churches. For the Catholic approach, there is deliverance prayer and
anointing, Deliverance Mass, petit exorcism, and grand, or great, exorcism. For the Protestants there is only one deliverance service. The closest Catholic service to the Protestant deliverance service is the Delivery
Mass. However, a Delivery Mass is performed only once on any given
day, unlike the petit and grand exorcisms.

5.3 NONCLERICAL PARTICIPANTS

At present, there is one thing that the Roman Catholic and Protestant
exorcists have in common. That similarity resides in the numbers and
types of people present during an exorcism session. Some differences
are present in the two spiritual approaches to demonic activity, such
as the use of two clergymen by Catholics. But, for the most part, what
is described in this section is applicable to both faith categories with
few exceptions.

It is a united belief among all Christians that prayer, regardless of
who is praying, is a powerful instrument against the powers and entities
of hell. Prayer is the primary activity in both exorcisms and deliverance
services throughout all denominations and schism related faiths. It has
been a long-held and perpetuated Protestant myth that Catholics pray
to God and Christ solely through their priests. Nothing could be further
from the truth, as all Catholics, from catechumens to popes, pray directly to God and the Holy Son, Jesus Christ.

In the process of expelling demons, a Catholic priest will invite
the afflicted person's family members and close friends, who are also
Catholic. This isn't a strict rule, and even the afflicted person may invite
people who are special to them regardless of the practiced faith of the

person. The importance is to have as many truly faithful Christians present and united in prayer over the victim of demonic attack as possible.

The afflicted person is either placed on a bed or in a chair that is centered in the room while the supporting participants form a circle around him or her. Each nonclerical participant is given a prayer and song book that allows them to act in unison and in appropriate timing to the prayers and demands made by the priest during the exorcism. Such a book can be as simple as a couple of typed pages. Protestant deliverance services are very rarely as organized, though.

None of the participants hold any special training in medicine, psychology, or theology except by pure chance. For the most part, doctors of medicine and psychology, even as practicing Catholics, will avoid such sessions in fear of being negatively impacted in their careers. The nonclerical participants all range from the parish secretary to the butcher down the street, and their roles in the process are restricted solely to prayer and response during exorcism sessions. Some may also serve to restrain the afflicted person in times of violence or attempts to leave before the session concludes.

Before beginning the ritual, the priest or minister will brief the participants. The supporters will learn such things as the importance of not engaging the demonic entity in conversation and to address it only with commands. There will be other things told to the group intended to make the session go well and to ensure that none of the participants themselves unwittingly take a demonic presence home with them.

What to expect during the exorcism session is often discussed, too. This prevents panic and disorganized fleeing when strange things begin to happen. Strange things will indeed begin to happen in a genuine case of demonic possession. A special blessing service and, for Catholics, confessions take place in order to protect each participant from the demon's exploitation of their guilt and vulnerabilities.

5.4 POST-RITE ACTIVITIES

A follow-up visit and evaluation is usually scheduled for cases where the great, or grand, exorcism has been performed in the Catholic Church or church of a similar faith. Such a follow-up does include some minor prayer, maybe praying the rosary together, and discussion on how well things have been going since the closing of the exorcism. Such conduct of lesser services are important in order to see if the demonic entity has or is attempting to return. According to the *Rituale Romanum*, this is known to happen, as the demon(s) may try to fool the exorcist into believing that the exorcism was a success.[6]

The post-rite visitations are also a time of healing and bonding for the cured and his or her friends and family. In some cases, a feast may be celebrated in joyful recognition of the person's deliverance from evil forces. In other cases, family and friends, along with the priests, may simply be glad it's over and be more inclined to rest and recuperate from the exhausting ordeal. Nonetheless, the visits are all purposed with verifying the absence of the entity from the body of the afflicted person.

Elements that are specifically examined during a post-rite visitation are the same as those examined for the initial determination of possession. However, since the medical and psychological possibilities are supposed to have already been eliminated through the initial investigative process, this examination focuses only on those signs and symptoms displayed by the afflicted person just before and during the exorcism ritual. The idea is to verify that the demonic entity has indeed left the body and is no longer entering or harassing the victim. When the priest is satisfied that the entity is gone, then the case can be closed and the final report written and retained for posterity in the church.

As has been revealed previously, most non-Catholic faiths have no requirement to document anything during an exorcism or deliverance service. Therefore, it is natural for the follow-up to be as informal and undocumented as the service itself. This isn't a huge problem for matters of spirit and church, as it is really just a matter of internal policy and practice. But, should a deliverance or exorcism ritual result in or be related to the death of the subject or any participating member, then there could be severe legal consequences for an undocumented event. It is truly mind-boggling to see how quickly friends turn on each other and factual inexactitudes abound when criminal investigators and lawyers get involved. This will be discussed in later chapters covering legal liability.

---

6. Weller, *Roman Ritual*, 2:169.

PART 3

Diseases and Disorders of the Mind

The devil is an optimist if he thinks he can make people worse than they are.

—Karl Krause, 1909

6

Commonly Confused Disorders

6.1 PSYCHOSIS

6.1.1 Definition and General Causes of Psychosis

T HE WORD PSYCHOSIS WAS first introduced in 1845 in Germany by Dr. Ernst von Feuchtersleben as an alternative to using the words *mania* and *insanity*. It has since taken on a definitive evolution and is now assigned to specific behavioral symptoms in both a primary and secondary sense. The term is a combination of the two Greek words *psyche*, meaning "mind" or "soul," and *–osis*, meaning "abnormal" or "abnormality." *Psychosis* quite literally means *abnormal mind* or *mental abnormality*.[1] Generally, the term is related to a person's loss of touch with reality or inability to differentiate between internal and external information.

Psychosis is actually a condition that is triggered or generated by an exceptionally long list of mental and physiological ailments. Some of these psychosis-generating disorders are discussed in further detail later in this same chapter. However, a general list of diseases and disorders is provided in order to allow the evaluator to key-in to certain diagnoses that may be discovered in medical records or through interviews with case essential people.

---

1. Beer, *Psychosis*, 177–200.

57

Cause	Notes
Bipolar and schizophrenic disorders	Schizophrenia (psychotic behavior that lasts for at least six months) and schizophreniform disorder (psychotic behavior that lasts for less than six months) typically cause auditory hallucinations. Delusions tend to be well formed and may be elaborate.
Drug and alcohol abuse	Intensive hallucinations can result from the abuse of alcohol and drugs or from their withdrawal effects.
Illness	AIDS, encephalitis, brain tumors, dementia, metabolic problems, and nutritional deficiencies sometimes bring on visual hallucinations and fragmented delusions.
Paranoid states	Delusional disorders might make people who are otherwise mentally sound have false beliefs that are paranoid in nature. Patients may believe the FBI is watching them or that someone is out to get them.
Severe stress	Psychotic symptoms sometimes arise after a major life stress, such as a pregnancy or a death in the family. Postpartum psychosis usually occurs a month after giving birth. Being subjected to violence also can trigger psychosis.

Table 1. Causes of psychosis

People who are experiencing psychosis are said to be *psychotic*, meaning that they are currently in a state of psychosis. Because psychosis can be treated and even cured, a person who has or may experience psychosis is not labeled as a psychotic person. This is used solely to describe a person who is actually experiencing or chronically experiences psychosis. Additionally, the term psychosis should not be confused with the term *psychopathy*, as they are completely different psychiatric conditions.

6.1.2 *Signs and Symptoms of Psychosis*

Psychotic patients may experience hallucinations, delusions, and thought disorder. The type and degree of hallucinations or delusions experienced by the patient depends on the psychosis-generating condition and other life experiences or environmental conditions.

6.1.2.1 Hallucinations

Hallucination is the sensory perception of something that is not actually present. A person may see, hear, feel, taste, or smell something that isn't actually present. The most common and alarming form of hallucination is the hearing of voices from people or animals that aren't actually there. Visual hallucinations can range from seeing bizarre colors to people who aren't actually present.

Hallucination occurs when the brain perceives something imagined as if it were reported by one or all of the five senses. In other words, the brain misidentifies internal information as external information. The person who experiences such a hallucination genuinely believes that he or she has seen the object and that the object is quite real. They will even pass a polygraph examination in many cases.

Visual hallucinations involve a wide range of experiences. A person may see colors differently or in more vivid detail. They may even see people or monsters. The old saying about "seeing pink elephants" is rooted in cases of alcohol-induced psychosis that involved a visual hallucination of pink elephants marching down the road. The experience can range from pleasant (as in a visitation from Saint Jerome) to horrifying (such as being attacked by monsters or demons).

Anneliese Michel reported that she saw terrifying faces often. She described them as being very physically real. She called them *fratzen*, or "grimaces." Other visual hallucinations involved seeing the Virgin Mary and her deceased grandmother. Here we see examples of visual hallucination resulting either from her epileptic condition or bipolar psychosis. What she imagined was being interpreted as real by her mind.

Auditory hallucinations involve the perception of sounds that do not actually exist. This is also mental misidentification of internal information as external information. In many cases, the person may hear his or her "inner voice" as if it were spoken outside of him or her. The most common experience is hearing voices that are disembodied. Some auditory hallucinations are simple words or animal-like sounds and others are more complex and commanding. The person may perceive the statements as being made to them or around them. For instance, a person may report hearing a conversation by and between two people who do not exist as if he or she were eavesdropping. In another case, a person may hear a loud, thundering voice commanding them to do something.

Again, the Klingenberg case is a prime example of misinterpreted psychotic hallucination. Anneliese Michel often complained of hearing the voices of Adolf Hitler, Nero, Cain, Judas, Reverend Fleischmann, and Lucifer. These voices tormented her and ordered her to do things that she would not normally do. She heard other voices such as that of the Virgin Mary and Jesus Christ. Auditory hallucinations, especially those where derogatory or commanding statements are perceived, are among the most alarming and scary of the hallucinations for most people who experience them. This is worsened when accompanied by equally bad olfactory or visual hallucinations.

Other sensory hallucinations involve the senses of taste, smell, and touch. A person may feel as though something is physically touching them (tactile hallucination) when no one or thing is actually present. To some people, the experience is so real that they will actually develop red marks and welts where they sensed being struck or squeezed. Hallucinations involving the sense of smell will cause a person to believe that they smell sweet flowery odors or rotting smells. Some sense the smell of burning wood or flesh. They may even sense good or bad tastes.

For Ms. Anneliese Michel, there were numerous incidents of smelling things that weren't sensed or perceived by others. Usually, she complained of smelling feces or something burning like sulfur. The only time others reported smelling the same thing was when they were informed by Anneliese that she smelled something. Such can be attributed to group hysteria or manipulation.

6.1.2.2 Delusions

Psychotic people may also exhibit delusional beliefs or constructs. Usually, these delusions are paranoid in nature. There are two types of delusional concepts: One is known as primary, and these are constructed at the moment under rather sudden conditions. The secondary delusions are those that are manifested over time. Secondary delusions are often very complex and designed, while primary delusions are barely comprehendible.

Paranoid delusions do not always include unreasonable beliefs of persecution. Some can include delusions of grandeur. For instance, a person may believe that he or she is the president of the United States while another may believe that they are some sort of saint. Then again, a person with paranoid delusional thinking may believe that aliens are invading his mind and the only way to repel them is by wearing a tinfoil hat.

The case of Anneliese Michel illustrated delusional thinking when she adopted the belief that she was suffering for the sins of others who were in hell. Another example is when she informed everyone that the Virgin Mary was making her suffer in order for her to atone for the sins of all those who have been sent to hell for their sinful lives. Additionally, she reported a belief that her suffering was for a higher saintly purpose. Such delusions are typical in patients suffering from psychosis but non-existent in people suffering from genuine demonic possession.

6.1.2.3 Thought Disorder

Thought disorder involves the inability to organize and comprehensively verbalize thoughts or ideas. Often the psychotic person will ramble, sharing thoughts and ideas about numerous topics like rapidly switching the channel on a television. In severe cases, a person may not make sense at all in spoken or written communication. Exceptionally bizarre ideas may be expressed and forgotten within seconds after being replaced with some new and equally bizarre thought or idea.

In some evangelical faiths, such behavior can easily be mistaken as "speaking in tongues." Speaking in tongues is a contemporary Christian concept whereby the individual is believed to be filled or possessed by the Holy Spirit, which causes the person to speak in an incomprehensible or foreign language. Although many observers have equated the event as nothing more than gibberish, those who have experienced it insist that it is a truly spiritual event. Some faiths believe that demonic possession creates a similar form of gibberish-like behavior.

Yes, this symptom was also observed by the neurologist, Dr. Lüthy, and psychiatrist, Dr. Lenner in Ms. Anneliese Michel. Dr. Lüthy observed during one of many visits with Anneliese that she was obsessed with the devil being inside of her and seemed to ramble through disorganized thoughts about the devil and a judgment of fire being dealt out to everyone. He remarked in his notes and testified in the 1978 negligent homicide trial that he did not believe that Anneliese was able to make any decision at that time.

6.1.2.4 Inability to Distinguish Internal and External Data

The primary factor of psychosis is not hallucinations as many people believe. Instead, it is an inability to tell the difference between reality and imagination. The brain, in a state of psychosis, is unable to distinguish between information that is internally generated and information that is externally generated and reported by any combination of the five senses. Associated hallucinations, delusions, and thought disorder are generated as the person struggles to make sense of his or her psychotic experience.

6.1.2.5 Movement Disorders

A person who is experiencing psychosis may also exhibit agitated or abruptly labored body movements. They may perform a specific motion or series of motions repeatedly for long periods of time before suddenly ceasing. At the extreme opposite end of the spectrum a psychotic patient may become catatonic and remain motionless for long periods of time.

Although catatonia is not seen very often in contemporary patients due to advanced medications, it was fairly common in schizophrenic patients through to the mid-1980s. A catatonic person may remain completely motionless and unresponsive to people for time periods ranging from a few minutes to several days or even months.

In the Klingenberg case, there are several examples of catatonic states throughout the symptomatic history of Anneliese Michel. Starting as early as 1970, Anneliese would go into motionless positions for as few as a couple of minutes to as long as several hours. The condition worsened as the young lady matured. There is a well-documented incident in which Ms. Michel experienced two hours-long states of catatonia in a single day.[2] Ms. Michel's states of catatonia included absolute motionlessness with the exception of eye blinking, whereas her episodes

2. Goodman, *Exorcism of Anneliese Michel*, 161.

of seizure would include repeated motions. Also, her seizures were short lived, whereas catatonia would last for up to four hours per episode.

6.1.2.6 Social Interaction and Daily Life Difficulties

Psychotic patients, especially those of the schizophrenic type, often have extreme difficulty adapting to new social environments and interacting with people not already known to them. Even when forced to interact they may simply stand and say very little. Unfamiliar environments will create exceptionally distressing levels of stress in a psychotic patient. Many psychotics are reclusive and rarely venture out of their homes; however, this isn't always the case, as some psychotics are able to function socially rather well.

In extreme cases, patients may become highly stressed over the slightest changes in their daily routines. They have difficulty in performing or maintaining daily activities and often require the assistance of family and friends. These individuals may appear as lazy and unwillingly to pull their weight to many untrained observers. In rare cases, people with schizophrenic psychosis may even neglect their personal hygiene and have to be reminded to bathe and brush their teeth.

6.2 SCHIZOPHRENIA

Schizophrenia is a mental health term used to describe a disorder in the brain that results in short-term (acute) psychosis or long-term (chronic) psychosis. In extreme cases, a patient may remain in a psychotic state until controlling medications are administered. On the other side of that status is a onetime psychotic event or an event that dissipates entirely with short-term and intense treatment. There remains a possibility of relapse with patients diagnosed with schizophrenia. This is especially so for people who discontinue taking their medication or take their medication sporadically.

Schizophrenia is broken down into three main symptomatic categories, which are positive symptoms, negative symptoms, and cognitive symptoms. These categories are diagnostic, and a patient may show any number of symptoms from any combination of symptom categories. The more symptoms present in a person the more certain that the individual is suffering from schizophrenia.

6.2.1 Positive Symptoms

Positive symptomatic schizophrenics will display behaviors that are simply not seen in healthy individuals. They lose touch with reality and will develop delusional beliefs to which they will cling even when faced with overwhelming contradicting evidence that their beliefs are false. Patients of this type often display the classic signs and symptoms of psychosis as described in section 6.1 above.

Numerous positive symptoms of schizophrenia are easily observed in the Anneliese Michel exorcism case. Hallucinations, delusional thoughts and beliefs, catatonic episodes, and even repeated body motions are all easily identified in the evidence compiled on the case for the time period starting in 1968 and lasting continuously through to 1976.

During the inquiry regarding Anneliese's death, Fathers Renz and Alt both stated that the injuries to her knees resulted from her repeated jumps from a squatting position that would last for hours. Anneliese's friend, Mechthild, found her one day kneeling, still and silent, in front of a little altar she had erected in her room. When she returned two hours later Anneliese was in the exact same position in front of the altar and did not respond to her questions.[3] This is just one of many examples of catatonia in Anneliese's short and difficult life history.

6.2.2 Negative Symptoms

Negative symptomatic schizophrenics are often misdiagnosed as having depression because their symptoms are so similar. Depression is entirely more common among American and European populations, and thus it is the first diagnostic conclusion made. It isn't until specific tests are conducted that the schizophrenic condition becomes apparent.

Negative schizophrenics will display characteristics such as a frozen face with a flat or monotone voice. They also lack an ability to feel pleasure in everyday life in a manner that is identical to that of a patient with depression. Negative symptomatic schizophrenics will often find it difficult to start or finish planned activities or projects. Generally, these types of patients will remain silent and speak very little with others even when forced to do so.

---

3. Goodman, *Exorcism of Anneliese Michel*, 161.

For Anneliese Michel, negative schizophrenic symptoms manifested in the inability to feel pleasure in everyday things. She confessed
to Dr. Lenner, her therapist, that she was unable to feel sexual pleasure or
arousal with her lover, Peter.[4] She often reported cases of not being able
to concentrate or focus on subjects or activities.[5]

6.2.3 Cognitive Symptoms

A person who experiences or displays cognitive symptomatic schizophrenia will often have difficulty in processing information. They will
demonstrate difficulties in concentrating or focusing, poor executive
functioning, and problems with working memory. In essence, cognitive
symptoms are centered on how the brain receives, processes, and uses
information.

Executive functioning is a term used by psychologists and psychiatrists to describe a person's ability to understand information and use it
to make decisions. People who display poor executive functioning encounter exceptional difficulty in making sound decisions or in considering information to formulate a course of action appropriate to existing
conditions or circumstances. This often leaves them completely dependent upon others in making the most simple of daily determinations.

The term *working memory* is used in the mental health industry to
describe a person's ability to use information immediately after learning it. Those who have difficulty with working memory may have to be
informed or instructed on something numerous times before they will
be able to put that information to use. This should not be confused with
a person's intelligence, as intelligence primarily concerns reasoning and
not memory. Working memory issues were not present in the symptomatic history of Anneliese Michel but could be present in any number of
suspected cases of demonic possession as an indicator of schizophrenia
or schizophrenic psychosis.

4. Goodman, *Exorcism of Anneliese Michel*, 53, 57.
5. Goodman, *Exorcism of Anneliese Michel*, 59.

6.3 DELIRIUM

Delirium is a very frightening medical condition that is usually brought on by serious illness. Patients with high fever, dehydration, or severe malnutrition may experience a delirious state. In the medical science community, this condition is usually indicative of a very serious root condition that has affected the normal functioning of the brain.

The most commonly known cause of delirium is high fever. In cases of heat exhaustion or heat stroke, delirium is an indicator of a need to immediately cool the body down and rehydrate the patient in order to prevent permanent brain damage or death. Patients suffering from dementia, discussed further on in this book, may also experience episodes of delirium.

Delirium is classified into three forms labeled as hyperactive delirium, hypoactive delirium, and mixed delirium. Hyperactive delirium is identified by the characteristic behaviors of agitation, restlessness, irritability, combativeness, rapid and loud speech, and hallucinations. Hypoactive delirium is exactly the opposite: the patient becomes drowsy, quiet, apathetic, and makes little to no movement or speech. A person suffering from mixed delirium often transitions between hyper- and hypoactive delirium with little to no warning.

The signs and symptoms of delirium include constantly shifting attention, confusion, rambling or incoherent speech, an inability to name objects or learn new information, disorientation, visual and auditory hallucinations, emotional disturbances (anger, fear, anxiety, etc.), disruptive vocalization (screaming, cursing, incoherent moaning or growling, or muttering), constant hand movements (pulling at clothes or bedding), and disrupted sleeping and waking. Delirium can and does share some symptoms of psychosis and could easily be confused as a temporary demonic infestation by an untrained observer or demonological evaluator.

Delirium is a temporary and treatable condition. Usually, this condition goes away as the underlying medical condition is treated. The primary medical causes of delirium are sleep deprivation, infection, alcohol or drug withdrawal, blood loss, dehydration, dementia, and hypoxia. If the delirium is rooted in a high fever then the doctors will work to reduce the patient's body temperature and rehydrate him or her. This automatically brings the patient out of delirium. In cases of dementia, delirium states are controlled or eliminated by treating the dementia with medication.

Delirium is often a red flag for doctors, as it usually precedes death in a number of situations, including malnutrition and dehydration. During the final weeks of Anneliese's life, she was obviously not eating and suffering from severe malnutrition. With the brain receiving little water and nutritional elements needed to function and survive, she quite easily slipped into what would be best described as mixed delirium.

There is evidence of delirium seen in the investigatory and trial statements made by the witnesses present throughout most or all of the exorcism sessions performed on Anneliese Michel. She was observed by Father Renz and Father Alt as having often transitioned from a state of anger and combativeness, mixed with screaming, growling, and cursing, to utter lethargy and apathy. The audiotapes of the exorcisms record these variations of delirium in Anneliese, too.

6.4 DEMENTIA

The word *dementia* literally translates to "loss of mind." It is different from psychosis, which relates a loss of ability to distinguish external and internal information. It isn't a disease in and of itself but rather a special combination of disorders and conditions that affects a large proportion of the world's elderly population. Alzheimer's disease is the most common dementia-causing condition.

The classic signs and symptoms of dementia are loss of memory, disorientation, communication and speech difficulties, abstract thinking, poor or reduced judgment, difficulty in performing simple daily tasks, mood or behavioral changes, misplacing articles, loss of initiative, and a marked change in personality. These individuals will display difficulty in recalling recently learned information or in the simple task of making a cup of tea. Episodes of disorientation can cause dementia patients to wander and become lost. Additionally, they may experience auditory, tactile, and visual hallucinations as the brain loses its ability to distinguish between what is thought internally and what is actually experienced externally.

Primary causes of dementia are numerous. The most commonly recognized dementia-causing conditions are Parkinson's disease, Alzheimer's disease, and Lewy body disease. Other causes include excessive drug or alcohol abuse, endocrine disorders, heavy metal poisoning, and hypoxia (lack of oxygen to the brain). Alzheimer's causes approximately 60 percent of dementias while only 10 percent are caused by conditions such as drug or alcohol abuse or endocrine disorders.

There are definitive risk factors for the development of dementia. These conditions include age, genetics, smoking, alcohol usage, and high cholesterol. For the investigator of suspected demonic possession or other activity, it is important to eliminate the possibility of Alzheimer's, Parkinson's, and Lewy body disease first. Old age doesn't automatically mean dementia and should not be considered in such a way. Longtime heavy smokers and alcohol drinkers should be suspected of the development of dementia as well.

On rare occasions, proportional to the total population of dementias throughout the world, psychosis can develop. This psychosis can be permanent or temporary and is most likely to occur in the advanced stages of such diseases as Parkinson's and Alzheimer's. In these cases of psychosis, the patient is most likely to experience hallucinations of various forms. Delusional thinking and beliefs are also common in dementia-originated psychosis.

6.5 DISSOCIATIVE DISORDER

What was once known as multiple personality disorder is today classified under the general term of *dissociative disorder* and under the specific definitive term of *dissociative identity disorder*. There are four types of dissociative disorder listed in the fourth edition of the *Diagnostic and Statistical Manual of Mental Disorders*, which are depersonalization disorder, dissociative amnesia, dissociative fugue, and dissociative identity disorder. In general, dissociative disorders are identified as conditions where the normal functionality of memory, identity, and perception are disrupted or hindered.

6.5.1 Dissociative Identity Disorder

Originally, this disorder went by a different name that is more easily recognized by the common person. What was once known as *multiple personality disorder* is today called *dissociative identity disorder*. One may still hear this condition referred to under the old term depending on who is using it, and *multiple personality disorder* is the most easily recognized descriptive of the condition among the general American population.

Generally, both terms describe the same condition, which involves the patient's displaying of multiple and distinct personalities. These different personalities are called *alter egos*. In order for this disorder to be identified and diagnosed in a patient, there must be at least two distinct personalities that take over the person, but many more can exist. The definitive conditions of dissociative identity disorder and those of demonic possession are remarkably similar.

In a case of demonic possession, a person is invaded by an external spiritual entity that has its own distinct personality. There may be many more than one demonic spirit in the possessed body who come and go. And, the personality that surfaces remains in complete control and acts in complete independence of the others.

In the case of dissociative identity disorder, the patient fabricates the alter egos. He or she invents them as a result of some disturbing trauma or in response to an inability to cope with reality or certain emotions. But, in a case of demonic possession, the person is invaded by what are believed to be very real and external spiritual entities. These personalities originated from somewhere well beyond the mind and body of the possessed person. One, dissociative identity, is a psychological response to a trauma, and the other, demonic possession, is a trauma.

Dissociative identity disorder is the most difficult condition to distinguish from demonic possession. Patients' behavioral and conditional symptoms are virtually identical and require careful and microscopic scrutiny. Until a concrete distinction can be made, diagnostic preference should be placed more towards the existence of dissociative disorder than demonic possession. This is because statistically one is more likely to encounter dissociative disorder than demonic possession.

There are some distinguishing indicators for demonic possession over dissociative disorder. These are the existence of human versus demonic personalities, existence of Aramaic, Hebrew, and Latin names versus names in contemporary languages, and region-specific names and/or personalities. An examination in these three categories tends to be the most productive in exposing one condition over the other.

6.5.1.1 Human versus Demonic Personalities

Generally, one is not looking at a case of demonic possession where any of the observed personalities are human in nature or origin. Demons are spiritual entities who were once angels before being cast out of heaven by God and the loyal angels. Humans and human spirits are not and never were demons and thus cannot possess a human body as a demonic entity. This is not to say that a human spirit is incapable of entering a human body but rather to say that demonic possession is demonic and not human in any way or form.

In cases where past or present human personalities are present, one must continue to lean towards dissociative disorder and may possibly want to examine the possibility of human spirit invasion rather than demonic possession. Spirits of human origin or design are less powerful and often less willing to torture their host even if they were among the most evil of people during their own times on earth. Human spirit invasion is even more rare than demonic possession because human spirits are weak and often incapable of maintaining their presence inside of another human body for any significant amount of time.

Dissociative identity disorder often manifests human personalities rather than monstrous or demonic ones. The names of these personalities are often of the same culture and language as the central, or real, personality. They do not speak in languages that are certifiably unknown to them as is often the case in demonic possession.

It is entirely possible that Ms. Anneliese Michel, the unfortunate victim in the Klingenberg case, was classifiable as having dissociative identity disorder. Of course, psychiatrists would have called it multiple personality disorder back in her day. She displayed several human personalities named Nero, Judas, Cain, Hitler, and Fleischmann. Only one of the manifested personalities was demonic and that was Lucifer. She spoke primarily in German and Latin, two languages with which she was very familiar and fluent in. And, whenever one or the other personality was present or displayed, her body was in its complete control.

The overwhelming number of human identities suggests dissociative disorder or psychosis more so than demonic possession. The fact that she, and the other personalities, spoke primarily in very well-known languages and not in languages more familiar to demons such as Aramaic or ancient Greek also indicates that her condition was not of demonic origin or design. There is little doubting that demonic possession was not the case for Anneliese Michel. Rather, there is significant and solid evidence that suggests one or more psychiatric conditions.

6.5.1.2 Aramaic, Hebrew, and Latin Names

In the case of demonic possession, the entities have existed for millennia in complete independence of the victim and the victim's language and culture. They will have acquired language and names of ancient rather than contemporary times. Therefore, it is logical to assert that a possessing demon will not be named Joe, Jack, Mike, or Butch but instead have names of Aramaic, ancient Hebrew, Babylonian, or Assyrian origin. Perhaps even Latin or Greek names and language would be present.

For a person suffering from dissociative identity disorder, the personalities will be more relative to the individual's native language and culture. They will also tend to be more contemporary, even if the assumed personality existed over a hundred years ago. For example, an American patient with Napoleon as his alter ego will speak in American English and use modern terms and slang. These are things that the actual person or spirit of Napoleon would know absolutely nothing about and would certainly not communicate with.

Again, an examination of the multiple personalities produced by Anneliese Michel reveals the spirits of people who existed in times and places that would have made their natural language considerably different than 1970s German. The only personalities that were German were Fleischman and Hitler. Out of those two, only Hitler could be expected to speak a type of German familiar to Germans living in the 1970s. Fleischman would most assuredly have used an older German dialect but, in listening to the recordings, he didn't. Fleischmann spoke in contemporary German.

Nero undoubtedly would have spoken in perfect Latin yet he didn't. Instead, he spoke perfect contemporary German. The Germanic tribes of the north were utterly despised by Nero and he would most assuredly not have chosen to speak in their language or anything evolved therefrom. Cain and Judas are utterly unfamiliar with the German language even as it stood in ancient times. But, as with the others, they spoke in 1970s German. This is something that just simply would not happen in a legitimate case of demonic possession.

However, Ms. Michel's behavior, as it has been recorded and is understood to have been, does not match either demonic possession or dissociative identity disorder. In most cases, people with dissociative disorder tend to have independent and distinct personalities that surface and are unaware of any other personality in or produced by the mind. Anneliese Michel demonstrated a full awareness by the alleged demons of one another. She even engaged in arguments and conversations between her demons. This tends to pull the situation back into the realm of schizophrenic psychosis rather than dissociative disorder or demonic possession.

6.5.2 Dissociative Fugue

Dissociative fugue is an exceptionally rare psychiatric condition that involves the person's loss of memories and personality. A person in a fugue state will leave their familiar surroundings and reestablish themselves somewhere else under an entirely new personality. This condition can last from a few hours to years depending on the triggering conditions.

The person forgets who they are in the fugue state. They will suddenly travel to other places unrelated to their normal lives. The travel will be sudden and unexpected by everyone, including the patient. The patient will not know who they are or have any memories of their past during the fugue state. Often, in protracted fugue states, the patient will establish a new life and continue on with life. Additionally, once a person recovers from their fugue state the memories and identity assumed will be forgotten.

6.5.3 Dissociative Amnesia

Many of the symptoms experienced in dissociative fugue are experienced in dissociative amnesia. The difference between the two disorders is in the cause. For fugue state to exist, there must be no disease or physical injury to the brain. Dissociative fugue is purely a psychiatric issue, while dissociative amnesia is the result of permanent or temporary physical injury to the brain. The patient may lose all memory and identity of the original personality while remaining capable of learning new information.

6.5.4 Depersonalization Disorder

A person affected by depersonalization disorder experiences sensations of not being in the body. It is often described as being an experience similar to watching a movie or of everything being unreal to the patient. The patient often feels automated, as if going through life without actually experiencing it. Others have described the experience as a feeling of being in a dream or experiencing some sort of out-of-body experience.

Depersonalization experience can last from just a few seconds to several days. It is normal for people to occasionally experience depersonalization or derealization throughout their lives. But, disorder is present where the episodes become exceptionally protracted or recurring. This is especially so where the quality of life is affected.

In the Klingenberg case, Anneliese Michel often described feelings of being outside of herself or being an observer rather than a participant in the reality around her. She would often inform her therapist and clergymen of not being herself or of being in a corner watching everything. These could be descriptions of depersonalization experience and possibly disorder rather than the effects of supernatural influences or exposure.

6.6 POST-TRAUMATIC STRESS DISORDER

Post-traumatic stress disorder (PTSD) is often associated with war and law enforcement veterans. However, it is also present in people who have experienced near death traumas, violent attacks, rape, and chronic child or spouse abuse. As the name implies, this disorder is caused by any number of overwhelmingly traumatic stressors in a singularly intense event or via continuous exposure to severely traumatic events or environments.

PTSD does not usually manifest in the patient immediately following the stressor event. Instead, a patient may begin to suffer the symptoms of the disorder months or even years after removal from the high stress experience or environment. PTSD symptoms are triggered by something that causes the traumatic event to be remembered and relived by the patient.

It is the repeated reliving of the traumatic event(s) that gives birth to the many life-disrupting symptoms common to PTSD. The patient may suffer sleep disorders, anxiety attacks, intrusive thoughts, phobias of places and people that serve as reminders of the original stressor event, irritability or violent outbursts, and a general emotional numbing. The recurring memories, also known as *flashbacks*, can generate such intense levels of stress that the person's ability to cope begins to break down. This is especially so when intense anxiety attacks occur without treatment.

Severe PTSD symptoms can cause a person to experience psychotic episodes as the stress exceeds his or her ability to cope. PTSD-induced psychosis is symptomatically the same as that listed for general psychosis discussed earlier in this book. The patient may reexperience his or her past traumatic history as the loss of distinction between internal and external information sets in. Hallucinations are frequently experienced by PTSD psychotics. Paranoid delusions are also common.

Research has also revealed that women who have developed PTSD in relation to early childhood sexual abuse often develop borderline personality disorder. Some severe cases will result in the development of dissociative identity disorder or depersonalization disorder. Patients who have been exposed to protracted and repeated sexual abuse may also develop schizophrenia simultaneously with PTSD.

PTSD is an important diagnosis when investigating and evaluating suspected cases of demonic possession or molestation. A person who is suffering from long-term and severe PTSD is at risk of developing temporary cases of psychosis that can cause a person to see and hear very scary things that simply never existed. The investigating demonologist or clergyman must eliminate the possibility of the simultaneous existence of schizophrenia, schizophrenic psychosis, or the development of PTSD-induced psychosis before a determination of demonic activity can be asserted.

6.7 BIPOLAR DISORDER

Bipolar disorder, also known as manic-depressive disorder, is a psychiatric diagnosis that involves an uncontrolled cycling between depression and mania. The term *mania* is used by mental health professionals to describe an unusually high or intense mood that is uncharacteristic of the person experiencing the elevated mood. Bipolar patients are frequently misdiagnosed with schizophrenia because of their symptomatic similarities.

The characteristic elements of bipolar disorder lie in the rapid and uncontrolled cycling between mania and depression. The two, depression and mania, are polar opposites, and it is this that gives the disorder its name and describes its primary life-disrupting characteristic. There are periods of balance between experiences of extreme mania or depression, but while very much appreciated by those who live with and around the affected person, these periods are usually short lived.

Statistically, onset of the full condition occurs during the patient's adolescent or early adult years. The disorder, in severe cases, has a profoundly negative impact on the life of the affected person. It is also a very stressing condition for the person's close family members and friends, as the mood extremes have to be endured and handled by them as well. Effective treatment is available through the combined use of psychotherapy and mood-controlling medications. Primary emphasis is placed on controlling the polar oscillations in the patient's mood swings prior to the introduction of psychotherapy.

The signs and symptoms of patients in the depressive episode include persistent feelings of sadness, anxiety, guilt, anger, isolation, or hopelessness. They may also experience disturbed sleep, loss in appetite, and feelings of fatigue or lost motivation. A bipolar patient in the depressive episode or cycle can also display general apathy and a loss of interest or enjoyment of daily activities or favorite hobbies. In some cases, the affected person may display a morbid ideology regarding suicide and be at increased risk of suicide.

When a person enters the manic episode of bipolar disorder, he or she becomes emotionally hypersensitive, lacks an ability to concentrate on things, becomes uncharacteristically giddy, loses the ability to make sound decisions, and acts in reckless ways. The person may become irritable to a point of being in a rage while others will experience feelings of euphoria. Bipolar patients may have a feeling of having been chosen or of being on a special mission. Other delusions of grandeur may also manifest in the manic mind.

Extreme states of depression and mania can produce cases of psychosis. In these cases the patient will experience hallucinations and delusions. For the demonic investigator, psychotic states, known in earlier times as *manic depressive psychosis*, is cause for further investigation in order to be certain that a suspected possession is not a consequence of mental disturbance. This is especially so where bipolar disorder is present without treatment or where the affected person has ceased taking medication or participating in psychotherapeutic sessions.

Bipolar psychosis, also known as manic depressive psychosis, is a prime suspect in the Anneliese Michel Exorcism case. Throughout her symptomatic history she expressed feelings of isolation and depersonalization, states of euphoria and then states of catatonia, and the delusional belief that she had been chosen for a special and holy mission by the Virgin Mary. Near the end of her life, she clearly displayed agitation to the level of rage, loss of appetite, and extreme displays of withdrawal followed by feelings of happiness in the extreme. The presence of visual and auditory hallucinations combined with grandiose delusional beliefs clearly indicates the probability that she suffered from psychotic states in both polar extremes.

7

Disorder-Causing Medical Conditions

7.1 MALNUTRITION

MALNUTRITION IS DESCRIBED AS the lack of essential vitamins, minerals, proteins, and other nutrients required by the body for normal and healthy functioning. It can be caused by a deficiency in a single vitamin or in the overabundance of a nutrient item. Physiological ailments can also contribute to the condition of malnutrition.

Nerve cells are among those biological elements that are most sensitive to nutritional imbalance. A multitude of psychiatric conditions can result from nutritional deficiencies, including psychosis. A good example of starvation-rooted psychosis is in the seeing of food on a table or of seeing an oasis in the middle of a desert where none actually exists. Psychosis under this condition is rare and originates from neuromalfunction resulting from a severe and protracted deficiency in key sustaining nutrients.

During the medieval days of Christendom, fasting was used as a tool to provoke visions and spiritual encounters with angels, saints, and even Jesus Christ. In these cases, the deliberate deprivation of sustaining levels of nutrients was used in much the same way as hallucinogenic plants were used by shamans of other belief systems. These things caused chemical changes in the brain that allowed practitioners to experience something beyond the realms of reality.

It was also believed that fasting purified the body. This is undoubtedly why the Roman rite for exorcism includes a statement that proscribes intense fasting and prayer to rid the body of demoniacal entities. There exists scriptural support for this inclusion, too. However, fasting for effect and starvation are entirely two different things, and it is of grave importance that the ministers of the faith remember this during exorcism and deliverance services.

In the last months of Anneliese Michel's short life, signs of malnutrition and starvation were plainly visible in her appearance and weakness. The recordings and testimonial evidence regarding this last period of her life seem to indicate that Anneliese suffered from multiple psychotic conditions. As her brain continued to struggle under conditions of malnutrition, she most likely did slip into psychotic episodes and more severe and frequent seizures. However, these conditions served as a further conditional complication rather than the central cause, since it is obvious that conditions of psychosis existed prior to her malnutrition phase of life.

7.2 SLEEP DEPRIVATION

In his 1998 article in the *Psychiatric Times* entitled "Sleep Deprivation, Psychosis, and Mental Efficiency," Dr. Stanley Coren writes that sleep deprivation and sleep debt can create conditions that mimic psychosis. He cited the cases of Randy Gardner and Peter Tripp as examples of psychosis mimicking effects of sleep deprivation. Dr. Coren also states that contemporary medical science fails to realize the full dangers presented to the human mind through sleep deprivation and sleep debt.

According to Dr. Coren, human beings, like other primates, require a certain amount of sleep per twenty-four-hour period in order to remain functional and healthy. When a person is shorted even an hour of sleep per day, a debt of sleep is created that can contribute to inefficiency and psychosis-like effects over time. Unlike sleep debt, sleep deprivation is the complete absence of sleep, which has more pronounced and intense effects on the human mind.

Mr. Gardner remained awake for eleven days (264 hours) in order to establish a world record while Mr. Tripp remained awake for four days (96 hours) in order to raise money for the March of Dimes. Both cases allowed professionals to observe some rather alarming effects of sleep deprivation. Both people began to experience delusions and hallucinations by day four of their vigils. They were also incapable of performing simple tasks, concentrating, or remembering what they were doing. By day eleven, Mr. Gardner had an expressionless appearance, difficulty engaging in conversation, and an inability to complete sentences once he began them.

Ms. Anneliese Michel reported to doctors and clergy that she frequently experienced phases of sleeplessness and interrupted sleep. Her episodes of hallucination and delusions were primary contributors to this loss of sleep, which may have been a contributing factor to the intensity and frequency of psychotic states and possibly even epileptic seizures. Again, this is more of a contributing or catalyst condition than the root cause of Anneliese's general psychosis and possible epilepsy.

The evaluating person may see symptoms of remarkable similarity between those of demonic possession and those of sleep-deprived psychosis. It is very important to investigate such a possibility thoroughly as the remedies are indeed very different and one is ineffective against the other. Additionally, it has been theorized that exceptionally prolonged sleep deprivation will lead to the death of the affected individual. Thus, a misdiagnosis of demonic possession may lead to long-term exorcisms that further deprive the victim of sleep and ultimately lead to his or her death.

7.3 HEAD INJURY

Traumatic brain injury (TBI) is a major physiological and often permanent cause of psychosis in about one out of every one thousand Americans annually. The most common TBI are contusions in the gray matter of the frontal and temporal lobes. This indicates that those areas of the brain that are responsible for cognitive and emotional processes are most vulnerable to the effects of traumatic damage.

TBI patients who have entered into a coma for any period of time are reported to experience some form of depression or impulsive anger behaviors following their return to consciousness. Also, for several weeks following a coma, a person may enter into psychosis and experience hallucinations and delusions. Long-term mental and emotional effects of TBI on patients have not been thoroughly researched, rendering little information regarding later development of conditions such as schizophrenia. However, there is some evidence that post-TBI psychiatric conditions have developed in people years after their injury.

While investigating a suspected case of demonic possession it is helpful to acquire information on any head injury received by the subject, regardless of when it occurred. The extent of injury received and any behavioral changes or mental deterioration indicators need to be assessed as well. The sole fact that a person has suffered a brain trauma in the past is insufficient to rule out the possibility of demonic attack. However, when the head injury is accompanied by a history of behavioral changes and other problems following the injury, then one may be looking at injury-related mental illness rather than true demonic activity.

7.4 ENDOCRINE DISORDERS

7.4.1 Hyperthyroidism

The word *hyperthyroidism* refers to a condition of the thyroid gland that involves the overproduction of the T3 (triiodethyronine) and T4 (thyroxine) hormones. These hormones affect every cell in the body and are of absolute necessity for normal cellular metabolism. The hormone must be rendered in controlled and balanced doses in order to prevent serious medical conditions from developing.

Patients suffering from hyperthyroidism are most likely to experience symptoms that are similar in nature to those resulting from an overdose of adrenalin. They will be nervous, experience anxiety, display tremors, and have a fast heartbeat. The person may experience weight loss accompanied by an increased appetite, intolerance to heat, hyperactivity, and delirium.

A very rare, but life threatening, condition known as thyrotoxic crisis involves an exceptionally high amount of T3 and T4 hormones in the body. Symptoms of this condition can include a high fever (104°F), tachycardia, arrhythmia, vomiting, diarrhea, dehydration, delirium, and coma. Without immediate emergency treatment the end result is death.

Because hyperthyroid-induced delirium is a symptom of a life-threatening condition and triggered solely by that condition, an investigator of demonic activity will either discover that the behavior subsided with effective thyroid treatment by medical professionals or the subject has expired. This condition is important to exorcists and demonic investigators in regards to the conducting of an exorcism rite. A person diagnosed and being treated for hyperthyroidism must be monitored throughout the process in order to ensure that serious complications relating to the disorder do not develop.

7.4.2 Hypothyroidism

Hypothyroidism is characterized by a deficiency in the amount of T3 and T4 hormone in the body. This can be caused by damage to or infection of the thyroid gland, failure of the pituitary to produce sufficient amounts of thyroid stimulating hormone (TSH), or a failure in the hypothalamus to produce thyrotropin-releasing hormones (TRH). Another cause of the condition is a deficiency in iodine. About 3 percent of the United States population has this condition.[1]

Early symptoms of hypothyroidism include poor muscle tone, fatigue, cold intolerance, depression, muscle cramps and joint pain, carpal tunnel syndrome, goiter, and decreased sweating. More advanced symptoms include weight gain, impaired memory, and even acute psychosis. Conditions of psychosis that root in hypothyroidism are very rare events. However, the possibility of its manifestation should be considered and eliminated during the investigatory process by demonologists and exorcists.

7.5 ADRENAL DYSFUNCTION

The adrenal glands, located atop each kidney, are responsible for the production of epinephrine (also known as adrenaline) and norepinephrine. These two chemicals are essential, in balanced volumes, to the body's metabolism and other neurological functions. Too little or much of these chemicals can cause a wide variety and physiological and psychiatric process abnormalities. A balanced presence of these bioelements is required for healthy physiological and mental functioning.

---

1. Jack DeRuiter, "Thyroid Hormone Tutorial: Thyroid Pathology," Guide for Endocrine Module, Thyroid Section, Spring 2002. Auburn University School of Pharmacy. http://www.auburn.edu/~deruija/endp_thyroidpathol.pdf.

People who suffer from adrenal dysfunction that result in low excretions of epinephrine often experience psychiatric conditions such as diminished concentration, depression, anxiety attacks, and attention deficit/hyperactivity disorder (ADHD). Those who have too much epinephrine will experience symptoms of ADHD, anxiety, insomnia, obsessive compulsive disorder (OCD), and psychotic episodes.

Those who have the misfortune of being afflicted with adrenal dysfunction psychosis (ADP) will often experience complex hallucinations, develop delusionary thoughts and beliefs, and have a general loss of touch with reality. Such are common denominators for general psychosis, and the condition may last as long as the adrenal condition does. Medicines are available to treat adrenal dysfunction. In most cases, the psychosis dissipates with the regulation of adrenal functionality.

A person diagnosed with adrenal dysfunction should not be automatically assumed to be suffering from ADP. This is especially so for those who are taking appropriate medications for the condition and have experienced no other complications related to or deriving from ADP. However, if the patient is diagnosed or suspected by medical professionals to be suffering from adrenal dysfunction and is not taking prescribed medications or other medical treatments, then one should consider the possibility of ADP and work with the subject in order to get him or her the medical treatment needed. The investigator of demonic influence is required to eliminate or identify the presence of ADP in cases of suspected demonic possession or attack. If this condition cannot be eliminated or is identified as being present in the subject, then a determination of demonic activity is not to be made as it is clearly not the case.

7.6 MENINGITIS

Meningitis is a very serious and life-threatening condition caused by the swelling of the protective tissues surrounding the brain and spinal cord. This condition is rooted mainly in the infection of the meninges of the central nervous system (CNS) by certain bacteria, viruses, and parasitic organisms. Because these tissues are beneath bone and above very sensitive CNS cells, there is little room to accommodate swollen tissue.

Swelling and inflammation is a normal reaction to infection. Unfortunately, the meninges surrounding the brain are encased in a hard, boney skull that doesn't give to internal pressure. The result is direct pressure on the brain that causes significant damage to nerve tissue. Left untreated, the patient usually dies. Late treatment will allow for survival, but there is usually permanent damage to the brain.

For the exorcist or investigating demonologist, the actual episode of meningitis is something that he or she will not commonly encounter as suspected possession by demons. It is the aftermath of the infection that is of concern. This is because brain damage, depending on timing and type of treatment received during the infection episode, can be the result of meningitis. Damaged brain tissue does not grow back or repair itself, resulting in permanent loss in functionality at varying levels depending on the extent of damage sustained.

Patients who have sustained brain damage due to meningitis complications will often display similar characteristics as those shown by patients who have survived traumatic brain injury (TBI). Both incidents result in permanent damage and a plethora of possible emotional and cognitive dysfunctions. Such damage can allow for the development of schizophrenia, bipolar disorder, dissociative disorder, and adrenal or endocrine disorders. Each of these conditions are known to occasionally generate acute or chronic psychosis.

A person who has suffered brain damage resulting from meningitis at any point in his or her lifetime should be evaluated by a cooperating neurologist or psychiatrist for the potential presence of psychosis or psychosis-generating conditions. However, the occurrence of said condition alone is not grounds to dismiss the possibility of demonic activity. The person's behavioral history since the infection must be reviewed and included with evaluative reports from assisting medical professionals. If there is a pattern or potential pattern of psychosis in the person's history combined with CT/MRI evidence of damage to key parts of the brain, then one must acknowledge the fact that the person is not tormented by demons but by the individual's mind.

7.7 PNEUMONIA AND HIGH FEVER

High fever may or may not accompany the medical condition of pneumonia depending on what its cause is. Fever is a condition that accompanies a wide range of conditions and ailments and has the potential to put a patient into states of delirium or acute psychosis. It is for these reasons that the two have been separated and addressed individually as subsections herein.

7.7.1 Pneumonia

Pneumonia is a medical condition in which the alveoli (air sacs that facilitate the absorption of oxygen into the bloodstream) are filled with fluid. The result is a reduced amount of oxygen intake that causes a multitude of subsequent physiological complications. The condition may be caused by any number of bacteria, viruses, parasitic organisms, fungi, chemical exposure, or other irritants.

One of many resultant symptoms of pneumonia is *anoxia* (also known as *hypoxia*), in which the brain is deprived of a sufficient level of oxygen needed for normal functioning. A person suffering from hypoxia may feel dizzy or light headed, experience fainting, become euphoric, experience confusion, and may also become easily disoriented. Death of brain and other CNS tissue will result if the person's oxygen levels become too low or remain at lower levels over long periods of time. In these situations, irreversible brain damage results, and the patient suffers a lifetime of emotional and other neurological dysfunctions.

In cases of severe pneumonia infection, a person may develop scar tissue that causes breathing and oxygen absorption difficulties for years. Conditions of prolonged low oxygen levels may develop, rendering the person vulnerable to the occasional psychotic or delirious episode. Post-pneumonia lung ailments must also be examined as possible root causes of psychosis.

Because pneumonia can be a life-threatening condition, especially for the elderly and very young, it is imperative for the investigating clerical official or other person to get a person suspected of having pneumonia, regardless of how minute the suspicion may be, to a hospital or clinic for examination and treatment immediately. In the case of Anneliese Michel, it is observed that she developed pneumonia, or what was suspected to be pneumonia, just weeks before her death. If this condition or any other medical emergency develops during the process of deliverance or exorcism, stop all activities immediately and seek medical help.

7.7.2 Fever

Fever occurs naturally in humans suffering from bacterial, viral, or parasitic infection. It is the body's attempt to kill the invading organisms or at least slow down their multiplication enough for the immune system to take care of the rest. At very high temperatures, a person's brain will begin to fail. He or she may lose the ability to distinguish between reality and imagination due to a state of delirium.

Prolonged high fever can cause permanent brain damage or even death to the affected person. The patient is in particular danger of brain damage or death when temperatures of 104°F or higher are present. Treatment includes the use of temperature-reducing medications and environmental temperature adjustments.

Any spiritual investigator who observes that the subject is feverish must immediately stop all exorcism or deliverance activities and immediately seek medical assistance for the affected person. Fever is not a sign or symptom of demonic presence but rather of biological struggle and must be treated by medical professionals as soon as is possible.

In the investigative process it is important to ascertain information on conditions of fever that may have resulted in CNS damage. If such a condition has occurred with the accompaniment of post-illness behavioral indicators in the health history of the subject, further investigation into the possibility of TBI-type psychosis is required. If this is the case, then one cannot say with sufficient certainty that the individual's experiences are of demonic or mental illness origin.

7.8 HYPOXIA

Hypoxia, also known as anoxia, is a well-known condition feared by pilots and mountain climbers alike. This condition exists when the blood oxygen level of a person drops below what is necessary to maintain healthy CNS and other organ functionality. High altitudes have less oxygen than lower altitudes, and mountain climbers often have to carry oxygen tanks with them as they ascend high peaks. Pilots, flying in unpressurized aircraft, are at high risk of hypoxia development at altitudes exceeding thirteen thousand feet above sea level.

Hypoxia can cause serious brain injury or death depending on the blood oxygen level and longevity of the event. In mild cases of anoxia, the

affected person will feel euphoric, experience confusion and disorientation, and have difficulty in performing simple tasks. At more extreme
conditions, the subject will become severely confused and disoriented,
feel weak, and fall into unconsciousness. Prolonged low oxygen level
states will bring the subject into coma and eventually death.

Severe cases of hypoxia with documented evidence of brain damage are grounds for further investigation in order to rule out any possible
earthly ailment or condition that may account for the subject's behavior
or condition. Experiences of mild hypoxic states do not result in serious
or permanent CNS damage and should not be of much concern to the
demonic investigator and exorcist. However, stroke, aneurism, strangu-
lation, and drowning all deprive the brain of much-needed oxygen and
often result in damage to the brain and other bodily organs. When these
medical conditions are encountered within the subject's health history, it
becomes important to have him or her evaluated by a neurologist or psychiatrist for the presence or possible presence of TBI-induced schizophrenia or bipolar psychosis. Such probability must be eliminated in the
investigatory process before any demonic influence determination may
be credibly asserted.

7.9 DEHYDRATION

The body becomes dehydrated when the amount of water excreted is
greater than the amount of water consumed. The resultant deficit of water causes the various organs of the body to malfunction or shut down
completely. Seventy-five percent of the body consists of water, with a
majority being inside cells and the rest existing within the blood and
vascular system. Water is essential in the bioprocesses of the body, including the removal of waste materials from the body.

The CNS is extremely sensitive to water deficits. It uses water in
emitting and taking up various neurotransmitter chemicals. Many of
these neurotransmitters, such as dopamine and serotonin, regulate
mood, emotions, and perceptions of the brain while others regulate thyroid and other hormone-emitting glands. In severe cases of dehydration,
the CNS will begin to malfunction, and the person may enter into a state
of delirium.

The signs and symptoms of dehydration include dry mouth, dis-
continued tear production in the eyes, discontinuance of sweating, mus-

cle cramps, nausea, heart palpitations, and light-headedness. The person may also experience disorientation, confusion, and incoherent speech. In many cases, a person suffering from dehydration will also show an elevated body temperature (fever) as the body loses its ability to cool itself. Without the prompt and proper receipt of professional medical care and intake of water, a person can and will die from this condition.

The condition of dehydration is not necessarily an important issue to exorcists or other spiritual evaluators in determining whether or not a person is afflicted with demonic attack. However, it is of grave importance during the actual process of exorcism or deliverance service. If, at any time during the exorcism or deliverance process, the subject or any other participant begins to show signs and symptoms of dehydration, the process must immediately cease and the affected person rendered water, at room temperature, and medical aid.

In the 1976 case of Anneliese Michel, the medical doctor who examined her body determined the cause of death to include dehydration. There is no doubt that had the exorcism team been properly formed and led by properly educated clergy, her symptoms of dehydration would have been recognized and immediately treated. Unfortunately, that didn't happen, and the exorcism continued until the girl died. The 2005 death of a Romanian nun during an exorcism is also believed to have been caused by dehydration and denial of other life-sustaining nourishment. These are completely unnecessary deaths caused by completely unnecessary exorcisms.

7.10 HYPERCALCEMIA AND HYPOCALCEMIA

7.10.1 Hypercalcemia

Hypercalcemia is a condition caused by excessive amounts of calcium in a person's blood. Effects of hypercalcemia include constipation, psychosis, bone pain, and kidney stones. Symptoms include fatigue, anorexia, nausea, vomiting, pancreatitis, and increased urination. Severe hypercalcemia is considered a life-threatening emergency as it can quickly lead to coma and death.

It is the psychiatric effects of hypercalcemia that is of most importance to the exorcist or spiritual investigator. Moderate and high level cases of hypercalcemia are known to generate depression, loss of appetite, and even general psychosis. An investigator or evaluator cannot determine demonic possession where psychosis or other hallucination-generating disorder exists or is suspected to exist in the subject.

7.10.2 Hypocalcemia

Hypocalcemia is the exact opposite condition as that of hypercalcemia. In this situation, the patient has an insufficient amount of calcium. This has a profound effect on the patient in severe cases, as they often enter states of delirium. This condition can also develop into a life-threatening situation for the patient, and immediate medical assistance should be sought.

Because delirium is dependent upon the continued existence of the triggering condition, it will most likely not be observed by the exorcist. However, the condition may be described as suspected possession by the subject or surrounding family and friends. Hypocalcemia can be a cyclically occurring condition whose resultant deliria become frequent in the subject. Untrained observers may easily mistake hypocalcemia-induced delirium, especially in cases where the condition has been experienced more than once, as demonic possession.

7.11 EPILEPSY

Epilepsy has a long record in the histories of both medical science and spirituality. For many hundreds of years, this disorder was believed to be caused by demons or other evil spirits who invade the human body for sinister purposes. The term itself is rooted in the Greek word *epilepsia*, which means "to seize." The belief was that an epileptic attack was the *seizure* of a person by a demonic spirit. To this very day, epileptic episodes are referred to as seizures. Humanity's exploration and examination of the finer workings of God's universe and laws has since discovered that seizures were of neurological origin and not spiritual. Today, cases of epilepsy that would have been considered demonic attack by the clerical experts of the 1500s are now treated with medicine and even surgical procedures.

A seizure is terrifying for those who have never observed one and for the person experiencing it. It is easy to see how earlier people would have mistaken this very earthly condition for a spiritual affliction. The rather superstitious and undereducated parents, siblings, and friends of Ms. Anneliese Michel certainly seem to have believed that epilepsy wasn't medical but spiritual. However, the better-trained and -educated members of the medical science community easily recognized her symptoms as being epileptic.

Members of the clergy are often among the better educated, too. But, their education and wisdom is focused more on matters of the spirit, Christianity, and other theological elements than on psychiatry and other disciplines of medicine. It is essential for every exorcist and demonological researcher to have and maintain a basic understanding of psychological disorders and diseases in order to better recognize and differentiate between matters of demonic attack and those of mental illness. Having a firm understanding of the most common signs and symptoms of mental illness is all that is really needed if a full masters-level degree in psychology has not been attained.

Epilepsy is not a disease in and of itself but rather a condition brought on by a vast number of neurological ailments. It can manifest in a wide range of ways and be triggered by another spectrum of stimuli. When interviewing a person, or reviewing the subject's medical history, it is important to key in on certain diagnostic terms.

There are two general types and over forty identified subtypes of epilepsy that present in a vast number of ways and degrees. The two general types of seizures are partial and generalized. These classifications are determined by the distribution of the seizure. A partial seizure is localized to a specific part of the brain while a general seizure is spread across several parts of the brain. There are at least sixteen subtypes of epilepsy, which are classified in accordance with both the originating part of the brain and the effect of the seizure.

All subjects of suspected demonic possession should be medically examined, with proper testing done, in order that the possibility of seizures can be ruled out during the investigation. In the absence of evidence eliminating epilepsy, evaluating clergyman and demonologists cannot accurately say that the person is suffering from demonic possession and not epilepsy. This medical condition must be among the first conditions considered and eliminated in order to declare a person to be afflicted with demonic torment. It is not enough that there is no history of epilepsy in the subject. There must be complete and recent testing and medical evaluation that concretely determines that epilepsy is not a possibility in order to move toward the acceptance of an event or series of events being of demonic cause.

7.12 BRAIN TUMOR

The brain is the center of thought and information processing for the body. For many, it is the central point where the soul resides, and for others the brain is what makes the *true person within the person*. Regardless of how the brain is viewed, it is the central information-processing center of every human being. It is a spongelike organ made up of specialized nerve cells that do not regenerate. And, it is protected by a boney skull, a three-layer tissue barrier known as the meninges, and a fluid called cerebrospinal fluid.

Brain tumors are a type of cancer that occur in the brain. They can be either benign or malignant in nature. Tumors can also be primary, originating in the brain, or secondary, originating from somewhere else in the body. Because the brain is so sensitive to even the slightest physical or chemical pressure or exposure, benign tumors can be life threatening. This is dependent upon the size of the tumor and its location in the brain. All malignant tumors are life threatening in the brain.

Cancer starts in the subcellular level where mutations cause cells to reproduce uncontrollably. In the brain and along the spinal cord, the cells that hold the nerve cells in place, called glial cells, can sometimes begin to reproduce uncontrollably, forming a growth or tumor. This type of tumor is called a *glioma*. Glial cancer is primary, originating in the brain, and can be malignant, invasive of other tissues, and aggressively spreading, or benign, localized, and noninvasive.

Another form of primary brain cancer is called *meningioma* and originates in the cells of the meninges. The meninges are located between the skull and the brain. The cerebrospinal fluid lies between the meninges and the brain itself. These tumors are primary and can be either benign or malignant.

Secondary tumors do not originate in the brain but from another part of the body. For instance, cancerous cells from a thyroid tumor may separate and follow the blood flow into the brain where they become lodged and multiply. The migration or spreading of cancer cells is known as *metastasis*, and secondary tumors are sometimes referred to as *metastatic tumors*. Secondary brain tumors of a malignant form are more common than primary brain tumors of both malignant and benign form.

Virtually all brain tumors are, regardless of malignancy, life threatening. The skull is perfect for protecting the brain from external impact trauma but a detriment to anything that causes internal pressure. As a tumor grows, there is nowhere for the pressure to go but inward. The direct pressure on the brain by the tumor or any inflamed surrounding tissue can result in functional disruption and permanent tissue damage. Eventually, enough disruption and damage can occur, whereby the subject expires.

There are several treatment methods available regarding tumors. The treatment applied is determined by the type, malignancy, and location of the tumor. Surgery, chemotherapy, and radiation treatments are the three main categories of treatment for brain tumors. Each procedure tends to cause damage to surrounding healthy tissue that can lead to permanent emotional, personality, and motor function abnormalities.

Psychiatric disorders can develop in people who have suffered brain damage from a tumor or any treatment used to remedy the tumor. There is an increased risk of acute or chronic episodes of psychosis. In some cases, depression and bipolar disorder may develop. In rare occasions, a person can develop schizophrenia. The type and intensity of the developed disorder is dependent upon what part of the brain has been damaged. Epilepsy frequently develops following treatment, too.

A subject who has or has ever had a brain tumor should be evaluated further in order to eliminate or discover the possibility of a psychiatric disorder. Psychiatric testing and neurological examinations by medical professionals should be conducted in order to ensure that the subject is not suffering from tumor or posttreatment-induced psychosis or other disorder prone to cause hallucinations or delusional thinking.

7.13 SARCOIDOSIS

Sarcoidosis is a most puzzling disease to medical science. Few people have even heard of the condition. The term roots are derived from Greek; the word is broken down as *sarc* (flesh), *–oid* (like), *–osis* (abnormality). The term literally translates to a *flesh-like abnormality*. Sarcoidosis is a

multiorgan and system disease involving the formation of granuloma-
tous inflammations.

Unfortunately, very little is known about what causes the disease.
Theories include genetics, infections, thyroid disease, and other disorders. There is great hope and optimism regarding the discovery of the
causal source as research continues.

Research has revealed that sarcoid disease is most prevalent in
Northern European populations. It is a disease that affects men and
women equally in all cultures. Occurrences throughout the world are
16.5 in 100,000 men and 19 in 100,000 women. In the United States, the
disease appears more in black Americans than in Caucasian Americans.
African Americans experience annual incidence of 35.5 in 100,000 while
Caucasians experience 10.9 in 100,000. The distribution between males
and females in America remains relatively equal. However, females with
sarcoidosis will develop hypothyroidism more frequently than males.

Although sarcoidosis begins in the lungs or lymph nodes, it can
manifest in any organ of the body. This includes the brain and central
nervous system (CNS). The disease can appear and progress very slowly
or it can appear suddenly. Also, it tends to disappear on its own for
many cases but can progress into a chronic systemic disorder that may,
in rare cases, be fatal. Effects on the brain may include the development
of epilepsy and mental illness such as schizophrenia or bipolar disorder.
Other sarcoid-induced adrenal and endocrine disorders can also lead to
the development of acute or chronic psychosis.

Sarcoidosis can be subdivided into fourteen types. These sub-types
are annular, erythrodermic, ichthyosiform, hypopigmented, Lorfgren
syndrome, Lupus pernio, morpheaform, mucosal, neurosarcoidosis,
popular sarcoid, scar, subcutaneous, systemic, and ulcerative sarcoidosis. The evaluator of suspected cases of demonic possession is most
interested in those types, such as neurosarcoidosis and gland affecting
sarcoids, which pose the greatest risk of promoting the development of
epilepsy, dementia, delirium, or psychosis in the subject.

In Anneliese's case, she began to suffer from malnutrition as a direct result of appetite loss related to depression and frequent epileptic episodes.
This certainly created conditions of dehydration and depleted nutrient
levels. Dehydration and hypocalcemia due to insufficient consumption

of nutrient-rich foods and liquids could have led to pre-exorcism conditions of delirium or psychosis.

After the exorcism rituals began, Ms. Michel was denied food and water in order to ward off demonic forces through fasting. Having already been in a condition of malnutrition, Anneliese's fasting would have exacerbated her condition, leading to more frequent and intense episodes of delirium and psychosis. As her body began to shut down and die, the presiding clergy and participating family members would have intensified their activities under the belief that the demons were being forced out. It proved to be a fatally erroneous interpretation of her condition and behavior.

PART 4

A Standardized Approach to Suspected Possession and Exorcism

Let us diligently apply the means, never doubting that a just God, in his own good time, will give us the rightful result.

—Abraham Lincoln, letter to James C. Conkling, 1863

8

Assessment and Investigation

BEFORE A PERSON MAY be determined or classified as a victim of demoniacal possession or molestation, there must first be a thorough
investigation, a reviewed initial conclusion, and an endorsed concurrence with the investigator's conclusion of demoniacal activity. The
process sounds complicated but in actuality it isn't. It is, however, a very
thorough and far more accurate approach to the subject than anything
implemented in the field of spirituality before. There are four steps, with
one leading into the other.

First, there is the investigatory and review process. Second, there
is the concurrence and authorization process. Third, there is the exorcism or deliverance execution process. Finally, there is post-exorcism or
-deliverance examination and determination. Each of these processes
consist of a series of standardized actions. This is known as the IREF
(investigate, review, exorcise, and follow up) model.

Figure 3. IREF model

8.1 DOCUMENTATION OF COMPLETE PERSONAL HISTORY

The acquisition of all possible information, in the form of written statements, letters, journals, and other forms of records is of vital importance to the evaluator as he or she goes about the business of piecing together the subject's personal and medical history. It is equally important to conduct interviews with as many relevant people as possible. Any incident of conversation or discovery that is not documented can quickly be forgotten or challenged entirely.

The demonological investigator must develop a compulsion for writing things down, using recording instruments, and making copies or photographs of related material and information, regardless how important things appear initially. The subject's personal history must be written with thorough support documentation. The investigator's activities throughout the investigation must be documented in order to illustrate the thoroughness of the investigation.

Every moment, or as much as possible, of the subject's life needs to be explored and documented during the investigatory process. The minutest of details can reveal much during the analytic phase of the subject evaluation. Be careful to document events that have had or could potentially have had an impact on the emotional, psychiatric, social, and general health of the subject. Disorders such as schizophrenia, bipolar disorder, traumatic brain injury (TBI), and psychological ailments occur or begin development during the childhood years for many patients. Although schizophrenia can develop and TBI can happen at any time during a subject's life, their existence in the subject's personal and medical history can shed light on what the subject may be experiencing that may have some cause other than the demoniacal.

The conditions or quality of life experienced by the subject during each part of his or her life are of great importance when evaluating the subject. Was the person raised in a stressful or emotionally abusive environment? Were there any traumatic events experienced such as assault, rape, sexual molestation, physical abuse, or near death events? Was the subject an only child or one of many? Is the subject an orphan or other ward of the state that passed from one set of foster parents to another? Who were the foster parents and what were they like? These are the types of questions that must be covered in detail for each part of the subject's life history.

The subject's medical history must also be explored and documented. Did the subject ever have mumps, measles, rubella, hepatitis, or meningitis? What treatments were used and when did the illness end? Has the subject suffered any traumatic or hard blows to the head? Has he or she ever had a brain tumor? Does the subject presently have a brain tumor? What treatments were used for the tumor? Is there a history of psychiatric illness? What medications are being taken by the subject and what are they for? Has the subject had a recent physical examination? Be as thorough as possible. Ask about sexually transmitted diseases such as syphilis and HIV.

The evaluator, or religious order supervising the investigatory effort, should develop and have on hand appropriate forms and other record-making and -keeping items. Today, the making of customized statement forms, interview reports, witness information sheets, diagram supplemental forms, and other standard documents is easy due to the advancements in word processing software and computers. However, it needn't be that complex, as a simple letterhead with typed information is just as good

Wherever possible and practical, the investigating person or team should conduct interviews with witnesses and the subject with audio or audiovisual recorders. Audiovisual recording is the better of the two but audio recordings should be made at a minimum. Before delving into the interview, be sure to state the case, location of interview, subject's name, the witness or interviewee's name, the date, time, and all persons present during the interview.

Felicitas D. Goodman, author of the book *The Exorcism of Anneliese Michel*, serves as an excellent example of a person who has conducted a thorough collection of documented facts uncovered by her investigative efforts regarding the Klingenberg case. Every element of the written history of Anneliese Michel's life has documented supporting evidence that are verifiable by others. She collected as much information as was available, regardless of whether it supported or refuted the idea of demoniacal activity. A chronological report is only as useful as the details it contains.

Reports of feelings or physical effects experienced by the evaluator shall not, when absent of other documented experiences by other people, be considered evidence that is either for or against the possibility of demonic possession. This is true also for any member of an established investigative team. Such experiences must also have occurred for people outside of the team in order for team experiences to be considered evidence. One important lesson learned from the Anneliese Michel tragedy is the fact that nearly all of the evidence presented to Bishop Stangl by Fathers Alt and Renz were incidents that they personally experienced. These reported incidents were absent of any other reported experiences of similarity by people close to the subject.

8.2 INTERVIEWING WITNESSES AND EVENT TIMELINE

8.2.1 *Interviewing Witnesses*

Witnesses are classified in accordance with specific traits such as cooperativeness, skepticism, intelligence, credibility, and mental health status. It is always ideal to have background information on every witness before conducting an investigative interview but, in reality, that is never the case. So, it is important to ask a lot of questions and judge the person's vocal testimony and body language. These questions are preliminary in the interview and are more about the person than the issue under investigation. The idea is to gain as much information about the person as is possible in order to determine the character, mental stability, and credibility of what will be said by the witness about the case under investigation.

Although judges have authority to compel answers and cooperation, a demonologist or member of clergy has no such power. Even policemen are very limited on how they question suspects and to what degree they can force answers. Therefore, one must keep in mind that any cooperation rendered by the witness is voluntary and may be ceased or limited at any time by that person.

In order to get as much cooperation as possible, an investigator should remain polite and not accusatory or aggressive in questioning. Regardless of what the investigator believes personally, there should be no show of disbelief, ridicule, resentment, accusation, or doubt in the voice or body language. The goal is to acquire raw data on the subject as it is seen and rendered by those who have been present to witness a possible demonic event. Care must be taken so as to lower all barriers to open communication and prevent creating new ones.

Do not attempt to push people into answering questions, as this only builds aggravation and increased uncooperativeness in the witness. An uncooperative witness will remain uncooperative as long as someone is trying to pressure him or her into talking. In these cases, it is best to simply hand the witness a card with the investigator's name and contact information and politely leave while stressing the fact that he or she may call at any time. Anything beyond that invites trouble and goes nowhere.

Interviewers should seek to first set the witness at ease and eliminate any tendency to withhold or fabricate information. Second, the investigator should seek information that provides answers or understanding of the *five w's*, which are *who*, *what*, *when*, *where*, and *why*. Be as thorough as possible and try to acquire additional information that will assist in the verification of what the witness is saying. This may include the naming of other witnesses. Witness statement credibility must be verifiable or supported by exterior information or circumstantial conditions.

Be professional in conduct and appearance. A person who approaches another while wearing a dirty T-shirt, flip-flops, and faded hole ctrown blue jeans will find themcelvec treated in accordance there to. Having unkept or wild hair, long and unmanaged or unclean pony tail (especially for men), unkept facial hair, and poor personal hygiene will quickly get the investigator shooed away. Those who wear unsightly jewelry or unnatural make up and hair color are also quickly judged by others as unprofessional or even disturbed. Remember, investigating demonic possession is a professional spiritual endeavor and not a vacation.

Be neat in personal appearance and wear a suit or semibusiness attire throughout the investigation. Speak clearly and in an educated and respectable manner. Do not use any form of street slang as this will build derision in those with whom you speak and will also make recordings difficult to understand. Treat everyone with absolute respect even when they are being difficult or rude.

Remain personally distant from the case, and record the facts as they are and without personal spin or interpretation. Do not ask questions that are leading or are designed to elicit an answer that can be interpreted in ways not intended by the interviewee. Remain aware of bias, and act so as to eliminate its influence on the data collection and interpretive processes of the investigation.

When conducting interviews be sure to record the entire conversation without interruption or cut-off. Videotaping the interview is most recommended but at the very least an audio recorder should be used. Be sure to have plenty of tapes or memory sticks available to capture the entire interview without leaving anything out. Using two recorders with overlapping recording times at the end of one tape and the beginning of another allows for uninterrupted recording of the event.

8.2.2 Event Time Line

The investigation of suspected cases of demonic possession requires the creation of two separate time lines that can be incorporated into a single life history. The first is a chronology of the subject's entire life. It should include all medical, psychiatric, spiritual, and emotionally developmental events regardless of perceived importance or significance. The second is a chronology of the events that have led to the belief that a possession is taking place. This chronological report includes everything that the subject and witnesses have experienced that leads them to believe that the subject is being tormented by demons or other spiritual entities.

8.3 PSYCHOLOGICAL INTERVIEW AND ASSESSMENT

In order to gain a full picture of the subject and his or her mental condition, it is imperative that psychological interviews and personality tests be completed. The rendering, review, and assessment of these tests should be done by a psychologist or other licensed mental health professional in order to ensure their accuracy. The results of these assessment interviews and tests will allow the investigator to gain valuable insight regarding the subject and whether or not he or she is experiencing any earthly condition that may mimic the signs and symptoms of demonic molestation or possession.

Psychological testing is an essential part of the elimination process regarding mental illness. If these tests indicate the presence of schizophrenia, bipolar disorder, severe depression, or other psychosis-causing disorder, then further exploration must occur. If these conditions cannot be eliminated as causes for the subject's experiences then the investigator cannot, in good conscience, determine the situation to be of supernatural origin. If the subject refuses to participate in these tests and examinations, then one is left with the sole conclusion of a nonpossession-related ailment or condition.

8.4 PSYCHIATRIC AND MEDICAL EXAMINATION

As there are psychological, or purely mental, conditions that may result in hallucinations and other bizarre behaviors, so too are there medical conditions, or physical problems with the brain, CNS, or other organs, which may present in bizarre behaviors or experiences. It is therefore equally important that medical testing be done in order to determine if any medical condition may be behind the subject's experiences and behavior. Such testing can include MRIs, CT scans, blood tests, and other examinations and tests.

These tests and examinations are also of great importance to the investigatory and determination processes of the possession investigation. If there are any indicators that the person may have a psychosis-generating disease, then further exploration of that matter must be followed If the aliment or condition is verified as present or cannot be completely ruled out then the subject is not to be determined as possessed but rather ill and in need of appropriate treatment. If the subject refuses to participate in these tests and examinations, then one is left with the sole conclusion of a nonpossession-related ailment or condition.

A general physical examination should also be conducted by a licensed medical professional, with an assessment or physical report being released to the investigator or investigating team for inclusion in case records and medical assessment by the physicians of the team. The results of the physical examination may reveal issues that may require further medical investigation in order to rule out all earthly causes for the subject's experiences.

8.5 POLYGRAPH INTERVIEW OF SUBJECT AND WITNESSES

The use of a polygraph to assess the honesty, or presence of deception, in a person has been controversial for many years. Even its use in criminal investigations and trials has been contested hotly. Some have claimed that the assessment tool can be purposefully fooled while others have maintained that it is foolproof. Other arguments contest its accuracy entirely. But, for the evaluator of suspected demonic possession or molestation it can be a very useful tool, indeed.

In cases of very deep psychosis or delusional thinking, there is a possibility that the person will show no signs of deception when questioned about his or her allegedly demonic experiences. However, these are exceptionally rare occasions and should not be a reason for excluding the use of a polygraph examination during the investigatory process. If deception is detected, then the possibility of fraud or conscious construction of information is very high. If a person shows no signs of deception but other information indicates, beyond a doubt, that the person is not being truthful or congruous with reality, then the nondeceptive results serve to verify psychosis of a deeply rooted level.

Witnesses to suspected demonic activity should also undergo a polygraph examination in order to determine if there are any points of deception regarding their statements. This is important, as some people will pretend to experience things out of sympathy for the subject or to assist in the furtherance of a complex fraud effort. It is important to eliminate fraud and verify the credibility of the witness statements regarding events relevant to the suspected demonic possession.

It is best if the polygraph examination is given by a certified and experienced polygrapher. This will assure accuracy in the results and render solid credibility to the examination as evidence in and of itself. There is nothing that says that the investigator, if certified, is prohibited from conducting such examinations. Being certified as a polygrapher and using one's own equipment can significantly reduce the cost and time consumption of this investigatory step.

Another important point regarding the use of a polygraph is that the rules of evidence and case law applied in criminal investigations and subsequent trials are absolutely inapplicable in cases of suspected demonic activity. They are, by all accounts, in two entirely different worlds. Thus, a denial to participate in a polygraph examination by a witness certainly can, and should, be taken as a sign of deceptive guilt on the part of that witness. Any statements made by the witness that cannot otherwise be verified as true or accurate must be considered less than credible or even false by the investigator.

In many criminal investigations, the police will ask a witness or suspect if he or she is willing to take a polygraph examination strictly to observe the reaction to the suggestion. The witness may have absolutely no intention of actually performing the examination. But, the person's reaction to the suggestion can tell an investigator a lot regarding the credibility of the witness and his or her statements. The initial behavior and reasoning for not taking a polygraph will often give away deceptive activities on the part of the witness.

The same tactic can be used by exorcists and demonic investigators. However, if a person is willing to take a polygraph, it should be carried out. The evaluator wants to simultaneously rule out deception and solidify witness credibility. The body language related to the mere suggestion of a polygraph examination coupled with the results of an actual examination are but a couple of the many tools to assist in this endeavor.

8.6 COMPARATIVE OF EVENTS AND POSSESSION CRITERIA

Chapter 19 provides a detailed listing of the accepted criteria for demoniacal possession or molestation. At some point during the evaluating exorcist's investigation, he or she will have to make a careful examination of the facts and current conditions of the suspected demonic activity in comparison to those behaviors and conditions that are indicative of demonic possession. It is of great importance that the evaluator be vacant of personal bias and subjective interpretation while remaining as objective as humanly possible.

The best approach in a comparative study is to make individual numbered listings of the facts and then examine the section numbers of the criteria listed in chapter 19 or make a numbered listing of the criteria listed by a specific faith's doctrine. A copy of the fourth or fifth edition of the *Diagnostic and Statistical Manual of Mental Disorders* (*DSMMD*-IV or V) should always be consulted in order to have a reference to full symptomatic listings for various mental illnesses and conditions. These three elements are the ingredients of a comprehensive study of both confirming and contrasting facts.

A three-column table should be created with each numbered fact listed along the first column, the second column should be used for *DSMMD* matching, and the third column for faith-specific doctrinal matching. Where either the *DSMMD*-IV or possession criteria match a specific fact the reference should be noted in the appropriate column and row.

Once all of the facts have been compared to the criteria of the *DSMMD*-IV and faith-specific indicators of demonic possession, the evaluator will see where commonalities and differences in the case exist. Where the table shows the presence of both demonic activity and mental illness, the evaluator is compelled to conduct additional investigation and research regarding the specific fact in order to eliminate either mental illness or demonic possession. In cases where there is only one criterion match from the *DSMMD*-IV, then the investigator is obliged to count that fact as indicative of mental illness and not possession. The same, but opposite, is true for cases where a fact matches only a criterion for demonic possession. Only those facts that can be attributed solely to demonic activity may be counted as supportive of a determination of demonic possession or molestation. Where a fact cannot be matched as either mental or demonic, which is frequent in cases of fraud or prank, then the fact may not be counted as demonic or mental illness.

As with a scale, the matches will accumulate and weigh in with one category pitted against the other. If there are more indicators of mental illness than demoniacal activity, then the logical assumption is that the person is not affected by demons but by his or her own mind or some medical condition that is affecting mental processes. If, on the other hand, the facts favor demoniacal activity more so than mental illness, then one may logically determine that the individual is being tormented by elements of evil.

8.7 THE INVESTIGATION REPORT

The investigation report is the single most important document produced throughout the evaluation process. It does not present any information under subjective leaning or slant and remains objective. All of the information known about the case, the subject, any witnesses, and all other conditions and circumstances relevant to the investigation of suspected demonic activity are included regardless of actual or possible implication or interpretive impact.

The demonic investigation report has a standard format that should be followed in order to ensure the inclusion of all facts regarding the investigation. It consists of a cover page, organizational identification and notices page, table of contents, and at least four parts. These four parts consist of the complaint, methodology, information, and initial conclusion. Other parts may be added in order to provide for a more thorough description of the case and its facts. However, argumentative or perspective supporting elements should not be included.

This report should be scripted in a manner and in the mindset of a police detective or forensic scientist. In law enforcement, the facts are whatever they are, and it is left up to the prosecutors, attorneys, judge, and jury to interpret them. This is the case for the demonological investigator, too. Remain neutral and report only the facts until the concluding part is scripted. The report will be closely reviewed and evaluated during the third-party review step of the evaluation, and those individuals will render interpretive conclusions.

The initial conclusion of the report should be analytical, with all statements being supported by evidence that is clearly identified in the text or in footnotes. Opinions or speculation is strongly discouraged, but where the investigator feels compelled to include such notes, he or she must ensure that these remarks are clearly identified as speculative or subjectively opined by the investigator.

An investigator, administrative assistant, or any other involved clerical or lay person is prohibited from allowing the public release of the report, or any part thereof, in order to maintain confidentiality for the subject, his or her family and friends, other witnesses, the community, and the church. Additionally, no clergyman, demonologist, para-psychologist, mental health professional, or any other involved party should reference the report or quote it in any manner whatsoever in any text without the express written permission of every single person mentioned in the report. Such quotation is and would be quite unethical and serve as proof of a striving for human aggrandizement or profit from the suffering of others (the sin of greed).

At the very minimum the investigation report should include the following:

1. A statement that the investigator was assigned to the case in question by the bishop, or other supervisory equivalent

2. A statement that the investigator conducted a thorough investigation of the subject, the witnesses, and all other matters and people related to the case in question

3. A summary of the methodology or investigative approach used

4. A statement that the investigator acquired complete, or as nearly complete as possible, medical and psychiatric records for the subject in question

5. A statement that medical and psychiatric professionals were consulted and that appropriate examinations and tests were conducted by these same professionals

6. A report of the discoveries made by professional medical and psychiatric examination of the subject

7. Observations of the subject by the investigator and other members of the investigative team

8. Attached copies of all statements, records, documents, letters, photographs, transcripts, and other items of evidentiary value

9. Attached time line of events relative to the suspected case of possession with a detailed narrative of events

10. Attached timeline of the subject's entire life history accompanied by a detailed narrative of that history

11. Attached comparative table of *DSMMD* diagnoses, demonic criteria, and factual conditions with detailed explanations and clarifying commentaries

12. The investigator's conclusion and determination regarding the case with factual support cited

The investigator must remain mindful of the need to include as much detail and evidence as possible in the report. Regardless of how the evidence or information may potentially be interpreted, it must be included. Also, the investigator's conclusion and determination must include acknowledgement of contradictory evidence in the case. Bishopric errors in judgment lay squarely on the shoulders of the investigator when a factually inexact or biased report is rendered and depended upon.

A thorough and objective investigation, accompanied by a complete and professional reporting of the facts and conditions of the case, will serve to prevent misunderstandings and erroneous decision making at the bishopric and peer review levels. Following a sound and orderly methodology, of the sort offered in this chapter, will prevent tragic conditions of the sort experienced in the Klingenberg case. There is no greater service to God and no greater damage to God's adversary than to act in the light of truth and with the sincere interests of others, both in spirit and flesh, at the forefront.

9

Third-Party Objective Review and Concurrence

9.1 REVIEW BY CLERICAL PEERS

WHEN COMPLETED, THE INVESTIGATION report should be given to theological or church clerics of equal stature and learning for review. Before an investigation is started, it is often best to predetermine who will be the clerical peer reviewer(s). This allows for a continuous flow in the overall determination process. When the investigator must hunt for a reviewing cleric, the process can be significantly delayed. Having a reviewing clerical peer assigned by the bishop or other clerical supervisor is best, as it precludes manipulating reports by the investigator through the use of preferred reviewers.

Clerical peer reviewers are qualified by being of the same faith, ordained, in good standing with the church, experienced in church doctrine and policy, and knowledgeable of basic psychology and the elements of demonology within their respective faith. Newly ordained ministers, though qualified to spread the gospel and minister to a parish or congregation, may not have the experience in such dealings as those of demoniacal origin. Therefore, they may not be able to effectively review and render professional opinions on the situation and evidence discovered during the initial investigation.

Clerical peers selected to review an investigative report should be critical and objective in approach. They should question the methodology, credibility of the evidence, and the strength of conclusions drawn from the evidence. Written requests to the lead investigator for points of clarification are encouraged and should be answered promptly and in writing as well. This allows the review to be documented and for concurrence statements to cite clarifications and additional information as necessary.

Clerical peers who review the evidence may elect to reject the conclusions of the initial investigation conclusion entirely. Under such conditions, the investigator may conduct supplemental investigations and research in order to provide additional information not previously available to the reviewers or discontinue the investigation and allow the case to go without determination. Allowing a case to remain unclassified is strongly discouraged, and reviewing clerical peers should be specific on what has justified the rejection. In most cases, a rejection is based on poor methodology, incomplete investigation, or overly biased presentation of the case and its evidence. Rejection should not be confused with a determination of a case being "nondemoniacal" in nature.

The review by clerical peers has several purposes and mandates. First, the reviewing clerics must decide, on the merits and quality of the report, whether to accept and approve the report. As was stated previously, the report must be thorough, contain verifiable facts, include an objective comparison of physiological and spiritual symptoms, and render an objective and professional conclusion of either demoniacal or medical ailment. The conclusion must be supported by the facts and evidence.

Second, the reviewing clerics must determine whether the facts indicate demoniacal possession or molestation. Generally, the reviewer is tasked with either supporting or disagreeing with the investigator's conclusion. The reviewing clerics may make a determination of demonic possession even if the investigator has concluded that the case is medical or fraudulent. In such case, the reviewers are burdened with supporting such determination with references to verifiable facts that are relevant and related directly to the case in question.

Third, the reviewing cleric or panel of clerics has a responsibility to evaluate the investigating cleric or demonologist simultaneously with the investigation report. It is absolutely essential that the soundness of thought and mental status of the investigator be verifiably absent of any mental illness or even demonic influence. The most common way to evaluate both the document and its writer is to request a presentation by the assigned investigator. Regardless of how awkward it may feel to the reviewers, questions must be asked that measure the investigator's grasp of reality and objectivity in the case. Such a presentation should be recorded in order that answers and clarifying statements may then be used immediately instead of the more complicated and time-consuming process of written requests and answers.

9.2 REVIEW BY CLERICAL SUPERVISORS

Following the conclusion of both the medical and psychiatric review and the clerical peer review, the investigation report, accompanied by the clerical review report and medical reports thereto related, are submitted to the bishop or other spiritual supervising authority for review, approval, final determination, and orders. No exorcism or deliverance service should be conducted without official authorization from at least a bishop-level official or higher. This serves to assist in the elimination of negligence or a failure in due diligence on the part of clergy and the church itself.

The bishop may, at his discretion, invite other bishops or demonological experts to review the information submitted regarding the subject suspected of demonic possession or attack. In reviewing the report, evidence, peer review comments, and reports from medical experts, the bishop has a responsibility to ensure that absolutely every effort has been made to expose an earthly reason for the behavior and experiences of the subject.

The bishop must question the approach and methodology, credibility of evidence, soundness of conclusions, thoroughness of the investigation and peer review processes, and accuracy of symptomatic identifications. He must also be absolutely certain that what is being reported to him is not, in anyway, influenced by anything other than the facts. Only then can the bishop make a determination of whether or not the case is of demoniacal or medical relation.

9.3 REVIEW BY MEDICAL SPECIALISTS

Because a significant part of the investigative effort and investigation report includes medical and psychiatric examinations and data, it is of great importance that the investigation report also be reviewed by medical professionals. These may be the same medical professionals who conducted the examinations and testing of the subject and others related to the case during the investigative process. The goal is to ensure the accuracy of the test results, the accuracy of the procedures used, and the soundness of professional opinions rendered.

The medical reviewer has the additional task of ensuring that testing has been thorough and the data sufficient to rule out or concretely identify psychiatric or other physiological causes for the subject's experiences and behavior. If the medical reviewer sees that additional testing or research needs to be done, then he or she will notify the investigator and coordinate with the appropriate medical professional to have the needed tests and analysis done.

It is not the purpose of this level of review to criticize or put into question the practices of any particular physician or mental health provider. Instead, the review should be aimed at ensuring that every possible earthly ailment or condition has been included and either diagnosed or ruled out in the suspected demonic possession case.

Where an earthly cause for the subject's behavior and experiences can be solidly diagnosed, there is no case of demonic activity. The medical reviewers' report, usually in the form of a letter, must include that the evidence has been reviewed, the medical and psychiatric investigation was thorough, and the results indicate no physiological or psychological cause for the subject's experiences and behavior before a determination of demonic activity can be made. In situations where there is an identified ailment, the report should include the diagnosis and be attached with the initial report and clerical peer report. The entire packet is then submitted to the bishop for review and comment as proscribed in 9.2 above.

In regards to medicine and church, a bishop should not counter the conclusions of the medical professional reviewing the case unless he has significant evidence provided by two or more other medical professionals to support the contradiction/objection. Only in cases where the bishop himself is a licensed medical doctor in the same field as the area contested should he act alone, disregard medical recommendations, and allow an exorcism or deliverance service to be performed. However, such bishopric action is highly discouraged for many reasons, ranging from spiritual to legal liability.

9.4 FINAL ASSESSMENT AND DETERMINATION REPORT

The final assessment and determination regarding a case of suspected demonic possession or molestation should always be the duty and authority of the bishop, or Protestant equivalent, in the church. The final determination report, written in the form of an official letter, is issued, or should be issued, solely by the overseeing bishop in his official capacity within the church. This is an official declaration that binds the church regarding the case in question and should be carefully scripted.

The declarative report should include a series of very clear confirmative statements and positions. The bishop should acknowledge and confirm:

1. That the church assigned an investigator of the suspected case of possession and that an investigation was carried out by that person

2. That he has read and understands the initial investigation report and its conclusion submitted by the assigned investigator

3. That he has read and understands the clerical peer review report and its conclusions as rendered by the assigned clerical reviewer

4. That he has read and understands the medical and psychiatric review report and its conclusion as rendered by the assigned physicians

5. The he supports or objects to elements of the aforementioned reports

6. That he, the bishop, has reached a conclusion regarding the case and what that conclusion is

7. That he, having authority to represent and act on behalf of the church, is or is not authorizing an exorcism or deliverance service for the subject of the case in question

If the bishop has decided that demonic activity is the root of the subject's suffering and that an exorcism or deliverance is needed, then he should include who the lead and assistant clerical exorcists will be. It is strongly advised that a bishop or other church authority not determine a case to be demonic where physicians or psychiatrists have diagnosed a specific condition that explains the subject's behavior and experiences. A case is not demonic where all earthly ailments or causes cannot be concretely ruled out.

In addition to the evaluation of objectively collected and properly reported information on a case of suspected demonic possession, the bishop must also carefully evaluate the mental and intellectual status of the evaluating clerics. If there is even the slightest doubt in the mental stability of the field investigators, then additional investigation should be carried out at the bishopric level to ensure a stable and objective source of investigative information.

10

Formulating the Exorcism Team

10.1 CLERICAL EXORCIST

THE CLERICAL EXORCIST IS the primary leader in the entire exorcism and deliverance affair. The exorcist is named specifically in the bishop's appointment letter and bares primary responsibility for the conduct and consequences of an exorcism or deliverance service. The clerical exorcist, also known as the *lead exorcist*, is responsible for ensuring doctrinal, moral, legal, civil, medical, and ethical adherence and enforcement throughout the process. The lead exorcist must be highly versed in demonology, satanic strategy, church doctrine, and faith practice. He or she must also be of the highest form of piousness, wisdom, age, and character.

Duties of the clerical exorcist include the overall management of the exorcism team. Scheduling and conducting exorcism or deliverance sessions is another chief responsibility as well as the writing of supplemental or progress reports for the supervising bishop. The exorcist also has a very important duty of ensuring safety and calling a halt to any exorcism or deliverance service in view of suspected danger of harm or illness to any member of the exorcism team or the possession subject. The clerical exorcist is not a "hands-off" or distant manager in these affairs but rather the active leader of the entire thing.

Presence and active leadership during every exorcism or deliverance session is an absolute requirement of the clerical exorcist. It is not safe, ethical, sound, or proper for the lead exorcist to be absent during any exorcism session. If the assigned exorcist is not able to be one hundred percent engaged and present throughout the exorcism process, then he or she is required to resign such assignment and be replaced by the bishop.

The clerical exorcist must be ever aware of the possession subject's medical, mental, and spiritual conditions. Not one of these elements may be neglected or treated with less importance than the others. Such neglect can result in injury or death of the subject or members of the exorcism team. He or she is obligated to listen to, assist, and oblige the professional comments, recommendations, and orders issued by the medical or psychiatric elements of the team. Where medical or psychiatric team members recommend an immediate stop to any exorcism or deliverance activity in the interests of safety and well-being, the exorcist must immediately discontinue the exorcism or deliverance service.

10.2 CLERICAL ASSISTANTS

There may be as many assisting clergy as the church may wish to dictate or is desired by the clerical exorcist. At least one is required as a part of a proper exorcism team so as to be available for the handling of holy items, relics, and books. He or she may also assist in ceremonial activities that may be reserved solely for those who have accepted holy orders.

The clerical assistants must be members of the clergy, must have at least a basic understanding of demonology, and be well versed in the practices of the faith. These clerics must also be of the highest order of piousness and character. Although it is preferred that the clerical assistants be of equal knowledge and wisdom as the clerical exorcist, they may be clerics who are in the process of learning demonic warfare but not at the absolute novice level.

It is neither the duty nor is it within the authority of the clerical assistant to conduct exorcism or deliverance services in the absence of the clerical or lead exorcist. The clerical exorcist must be present and performing in the spiritual leadership capacity in order to ensure appropriate actions and conduct occurs. Clerical assistants are primarily responsible for assisting in prayers, preparing the mass or service items, and maintaining all holy items and class-two relics. The clerical assistant may also hold holy texts in order for the clerical exorcist to read prayers or gospels as part of the church-sanctioned ritual of exorcism or deliverance.

10.3 EVENT RECORDER

The event recorder is an extremely important member of the exorcism team, as this person is primarily responsible for maintaining records on everything that happens throughout the entire exorcism process. He or she operates all video and audio recording equipment, keeps notes, types daily activity logs and reports, maintains security of all media and records, and generates transcriptions of all audio recordings.

The event recorder is a super-secretary and not a person of mere receptionist experience. The most effective person for this team position is a person who has worked as a court reporter or paralegal for a minimum of seven years continuously and without more than two years break from the last incidence of practice. Formal training in secretarial, stenographic, or paralegal science is an absolute requirement. This position should never be trusted to anyone less than a very experienced and formally trained professional.

The exorcism or deliverance team is utterly incomplete and ineffective without a well-trained, highly experienced, and talented recorder. The event recorder is the clerical exorcist's right-hand person for the collecting, organizing, and presentation of data regarding an exorcism or deliverance process. No details should be overlooked or misreported under any circumstances, as this data is what is presented to the bishop and may even serve in an evidentiary capacity for research or legal proceedings.

He or she is also the primary custodian of these very sensitive documents and data. Security of the data is as important as the accuracy of the data. Careless handling of media and typed reports or notes could result in a violation of confidentiality standard proscribed in section 13.3 of this book.

10.4 PSYCHOLOGIST OR THERAPIST

There should be at least one psychologist, psychiatrist, psychotherapist, or other formally educated and appropriately licensed therapist or counselor assigned to the exorcism or deliverance team. This individual, or subteam of individuals, must have a minimum of a masters degree in psychology or counseling, other than spiritual or theological, and be licensed to practice psychotherapy or mental health science in the specific country and state in which the physical exorcism or deliverance ritual is taking place. In addition, this professional should have a significant amount of experience in dealing with cases of psychosis, dementia, delirium, schizophrenia, and bipolar disorder.

The role of the therapist or psychologist is to observe the subject and the ritual participants, including the clerical exorcist, throughout the process of any exorcism session. He or she is responsible for monitoring behavior and other mental health indicators in order to ensure that the exorcism or deliverance service does not create a mentally harmful environment for the subject of the possession or any other participating person. At any point, where the therapist team member observes events or conditions harmful to the subject or the participants of the ritual, the therapist is obligated to immediately order a halt to the exorcism ritual or deliverance service.

In selecting and accepting a professional such as a psychologist or psychiatrist into the exorcism or deliverance team, it is not necessary that he or she be absolute believers in any religion or the existence of demonic entities but that he or she is open to the concept as a sociological process experienced by individuals. In fact, participation as a member of an exorcism or deliverance team affords psychologists, therapists, and psychiatrists an opportunity to observe a very real social experience by a very real individual mind.

10.5 MEDICAL SUPPORT AND MONITORING

The best people to enlist and assign to the exorcism team for the purpose of medically monitoring the subject of the exorcism or deliverance is not a general practice doctor or psychiatrist. The best possible professional for this post is a physician who is certified and possesses considerable experience in emergency room or urgent care medicine. These individuals are capable of recognizing even the minutest of conditions that are indicative of human health crisis. They are also well versed in how to treat a condition and stabilize the subject sufficiently for emergency transport to and care at a hospital. Emergency room/urgent care (ER/

UC) physicians, ER/UC registered nurses, and paramedics, with current licensure and experience in practice, can all serve to fill this most important position in the team.

The duties of the medical support team members are to maintain constant observation of the subject and to ensure that all vital signs and other physiological processes remain within tolerable levels. This person, or subteam of professionals, is also the primary responder to any medical emergency that occurs during any exorcism session and has full authority to disrupt and order a halt to the exorcism or deliverance ritual in order to prevent harm and treat injury or illness.

A bishop, or religious equivalent in the Protestant faiths, should never allow an exorcism or deliverance to take place when there are no medical monitoring and response elements included in the exorcism or deliverance team. The clerical exorcist, if he or she chooses to go forward in absence of medical support, should do so knowing full well the possible consequences to the subject of the ritual or members of the team and be willing to assume full legal and spiritual responsibility for any harm or death that befalls anyone of the team or of the subject. In fact, the clerical leader of any exorcism or deliverance acknowledges the assumption of full responsibility for the consequences by proceeding without professional medical support being present.

10.6 RELIGIOUS SUPPORT ELEMENT

The religious support element consists of as many people of the same faith or from the family of the subject as can be safely mustered into the place where the exorcism is to take place. These individuals must be selected based upon their faith in God, their love for the afflicted person, their soundness of mind and bodily health, their being baptized, and their willingness to see the effort through for as long as it may take to eject the demons that torment the body, mind, and soul of the afflicted. Those who are not serious in their faith and determination under the grace of God are in danger of being attacked or possessed themselves. Therefore, each member of this element must be closely evaluated and interviewed. They must be sincere at heart.

The duty of the religious supporter is to participate in spiritual meditation, prayer, and chanting or singing of holy hymns or prayers. Participation in scriptural readings and in other ritual practices is an important product of this role in the process of exorcism and deliverance. The religious supporters, along with the clerical exorcist, and clerical assistants make up the circle of faith that surrounds the afflicted subject of the exorcism. A weak link in this chain may result in a demon's wreaking havoc and mayhem upon everyone present. It is critical that each person be anointed and blessed accordingly.

10.7 THE ROLE OF SCIENTISTS IN A RELIGIOUS CEREMONY

It is often difficult to attract scientific and medical science professionals to the concept of assisting or even observing a possession evaluation or exorcism ritual. But this is mainly due to years of conflict between religion and scientific discovery, conflict that has been encouraged by the Roman Catholic Church's superstitious practices and rejection of any new approach to an infinite and omnipotent presence. It is also rooted in the "exorcism for show and profit" conducted by evangelical Christians located primarily inside the United States. But, science and Christianity are not enemies.

Science and Christianity do indeed have the ability to coexist in harmony. In fact, that is exactly what they are intended to do. It is the interpretations and rigidity of humanity that makes them polarized opponents. God is what is. God has created the things that exist and the things that bind and make work those things that exist. God has even made the planes of existence.

The priests accept what the Lord has done and ordered at face value and are thankful without need of details. But, the scientist is a priest of his or her own sort. As one preaches that all has been made by the one true God and through God all that is does as is done, the other exposes the greatness of God through the inner workings of what exists and how what exists interact. One accepts what the other observes as the greatness of the Lord, God Almighty. Science does not deny the existence and greatness of God but rather defines God's greatness and existence.

Nowhere will one find a scientist claiming to have invented physics, invented the cells and their processes, or of having created the atoms that make up all matter. What astronomer has claimed to have created the planets that orbit the sun or the moon that orbits the earth? Instead, one hears the scientists say that they have discovered these things. They have discovered what was taking place before our very eyes, one and all, for as long as God has had them in place. God, the creator, invented and built these things, scientists have discovered and defined them, and priests have praised and glorified God for it. These two, science and Christianity, are interconnected, whether some members of one or the other group like it or not.

11

Pre-exorcism Activities

11.1 PHYSICAL AND MENTAL FITNESS

11.1.1 Physical Fitness

THE CONCERN OF PHYSICAL fitness is all encompassing. Definitely, the fitness of the subject is of utmost concern, as an exorcism, or deliverance service, can be very draining and exhausting to the afflicted. It is vital that the person be given a thorough physical examination and be determined by a medical doctor to be fit enough to undergo such an ordeal. Of specific importance are the subject's cardiac, pulmonary, neurological, and renal fitness; blood pressure; and diabetic condition.

A subject can undergo an exorcism with conditions such as epilepsy or diabetes. However, the medical support element of the exorcism team must be prepared for complications related to these disorders and pay special attention to diagnostic and monitoring methods and equipment. Additionally, all planning and timing of eating and other breaks must incorporate the special needs dictated by the subject's health condition.

These same conditions and accommodations must be made for the members of the exorcism team as well. There are a plethora of incidents where one of the exorcism support people experienced a heart attack or a diabetes-related health crisis. This is an event that one would naturally seek to prevent from happening. Therefore, at the very minimum, the members of the team should have a medical physical that is no more than twelve months old and be determined, in writing, by their primary care physician to be fit to participate in the exorcism or deliverance rituals.

As with the other members of the team, the assigned clerical exorcist must also be of the best possible fitness for conducting the ritual and managing the team. Additionally, there are reported incidents where the exorcist has either died or been hospitalized from heart attack or stroke. The assigning bishop must ensure that the cleric appointed as the exorcist in the case has been medically examined and determined to be physically fit enough to conduct the ritual or service and manage the team.

The exorcism of demonic entities can expose the entire team to some of the strangest and most dangerous environments known to humanity. Demons have no love for humans and will, when directly engaged, lash out. Many of the most terrifying and violent experiences recorded in the history of humanity have come from encounters with demonic entities. The entire team must be capable of physically enduring both the possessed and what lashes out from within the possessed.

11.1.2 Mental Fitness

The tragedy of the Anneliese Michel exorcism case functions as a tremendous example of what happens when the mentally ill are treated as if possessed. The result is horrible and irreversible injury or even death. Anneliese Michel wasn't the first to die due to misdiagnosis of a spiritual condition over a physiological or psychological condition, and she certainly isn't the last. Sadly, a death occurred during an exorcism as recently as 2005 in an Eastern European convent. Ms. Michel's case just happens to be one of the exceptionally few well-documented cases.

Ms. Michel was not only mentally ill, but it is strongly suspected that at least one of the assigned exorcists, Father Alt, also suffered from delusional thinking and may have even experienced hallucinations in his past.[1] It is critically important that not only the subject of the exorcism or deliverance ritual be tested and deemed sound to undergo such an activity but that the exorcist is also sound of mind. If both the exorcist and the subject are mentally ill, they will certainly feed off of each other's delusions, resulting in a true and utter catastrophe.

1. Goodman, *Exorcism of Anneliese Michel*, 43.

It is insufficient that the exorcist candidate, either verbally or in written form, has declared him- or herself to be sound of mind and body. Such self-declaration must be supported by medical and psychiatric assessment rendered in writing and held in the minister's file. The assigning bishop must be familiar with the individual he considers to be best for the position and task. The assigned exorcist must be of sound mind, good physical health, great moral character, and pious in ways and practices.

This is also applicable to every other participant of the rite. If there is even the slightest doubt in the moral character or soundness of mind regarding an individual, then that person should be excluded from the exorcism team and barred from the area during sessions. Weak-minded and mentally vulnerable people can be affected quickly by dark entities. It is reckless to expose such a person to the likes of an exorcism or deliverance, as it places him or her and the rest of the team in a dangerous situation.

11.2 WILLINGNESS AND CONSENT OF THE SUBJECT

In order for the exorcism to be successful, the afflicted person must want and ask for help. He or she must be a willing and consenting participant in the entire process. The afflicted person has the right to withdraw his or her willingness and consent at any time. It is ethically, morally, and legally wrong to force any person into an exorcism ritual. Any priest, minister, exorcist, demonologist, or other person who does this to another is guilty of a crime against both the laws of God and those of humanity, making that person subject to prosecution and judgment in both realms.

A responsible exorcist and assistants will make certain that the afflicted person is fully informed of what demonic possession is, what exorcism is, what he or she should expect to happen, the risks involved, and what is expected of him or her during the process. They should know of and be fully consenting to the use of restraint by others or safe devices. The subject must be fully informed and aware of all aspects of the exorcism or deliverance process and have all questions or concerns answered to his or her satisfaction and understanding before proceeding with any exorcism or deliverance. Above all, the subject must know that he or she has the right to withdraw consent and participation at any time throughout the process.

Additionally, there should be absolutely no presence of pressure or coercion regarding the subject's willingness to undergo exorcism or deliverance service. Yet one psychiatrist did just that. Psychiatrist M. Scott Peck, wrote in one of his books about a person he named "Jersey." He originally diagnosed the young lady with schizophrenia[2] but then changed his conclusion to demonic possession after speaking with Mr. Malachi Martin over the phone.[3] It appears that the good doctor abandoned all of his professional training and experience in favor of diabolic possession, and what would be clearly seen as a psychotic episode or condition by all other mental health professionals was now a demon speaking through the young girl.

Between visits by Dr. Peck, a psychological evaluation was made of Jersey that included a report of behavior similar to that of a person who suffers from petit mal epilepsy. Although the reporting psychologist made a statement of not being sure that Jersey was suffering from epilepsy, the symptomatic characteristics of it were certainly observed. The possible presence of epilepsy and Dr. Peck's initial assessment of schizophrenic psychosis are of exceptional similarity to the conditions believed to be present in Anneliese Michel by medical professionals in 1976.

How Dr. Peck handles this patient is appalling at best, in that he tells Jersey, or whoever she really is, that she can either undergo exorcism or be committed in a state mental institution against her will.[4] Dr. Peck, with coconspirator, Dr. Lieberman, entered the hospital (under the guise of consultant) in which Jersey had been committed after a suicide attempt. She demanded to be released, and Dr. Peck simply made it clear that she would be held against her will as she was seen as too sick to be released but that she could partake in an exorcism in Connecticut and be released right away.[5] There is no greater violation of Christian, moral, legal, or professional ethics than to abuse one's position and authority—to violate a patient's trust—than to force a person to participate in or do something that he or she is unwilling to do under threat of false committal or imprisonment.

This is a horridly unlawful and immoral deed to which Dr. Peck appears to have confessed in his book. The exorcism could not possibly

2. Peck, *Glimpses of the Devil*, 28.
3. Peck, *Glimpses of the Devil*, 31.
4. Peck, *Glimpses of the Devil*, 39–42.
5. Peck, *Glimpses of the Devil*, 39.

succeed without the outcry and willingness of the subject. No matter how sad it is or how much one's heart goes out to the subject, an exorcism will not work if the subject is unwilling to participate and is, as Jersey stated in one of her interviews with Dr. Peck, a willing accomplice to demonic forces.[6] There is an old saying that relates to this type of situation: "you can lead a horse to water but you can't make it drink."

11.3 WILLINGNESS AND CONSENT OF THE PARTICIPANTS

It is important that each participant be completely willing and consenting to participate as a member of the exorcism team. The participants must be fully informed of the process, what to expect, what their function will be and what could happen during every exorcism or deliverance session. They must willfully accept their role and the risk that comes with their actions in the process. They, like all humans, have the right to withdraw their willingness and consent at any time throughout the process.

When fear compels any member of the team to leave, then let them leave without hindrance or harm. If one or more should leave to seek help for any reason, then let them do so without hindrance or harm. In many cases, one or more team members may become overwhelmed with feelings of fear. This is normal and often the result of demonic attack than of a lack personal courage. Once away from the influence, people will often regain themselves and return to continue the fight. But, under no circumstances should any person be forced to stay or do anything that they are not fully willing and consenting to do.

11.4 CLERICAL PREPARATION IN ACCORDANCE WITH FAITH

11.4.1 Roman Catholic

The Roman Catholic Church has the only known organized and officially endorsed written procedure for exorcism, called the *Rituale Romanum* (*Roman Ritual*). This text was originally written and published in 1614 AD by Pope Paul V. In 1752, the *Rituale Romanum* underwent a revision under the orders of Pope Benedict XIV. The Second Ecumenical Council of the Vatican, through which all of the major books and rituals of the

---

6. Peck, *Glimpses of the Devil*, 29.

church underwent review and revision, opened in 1962 and concluded in 1964 with a new, two-volume *Roman Rite*. The two-volume version was published in 1976, the same year as Anneliese Michel's death during exorcism rituals of the older form.

What isn't very well known by the public is that prior to the book published by Pope Paul V in 1614 AD, there were a number of other Roman Catholic ritual works in use. These were written by various bishops throughout the world. Additionally, when Pope Paul V published the *Roman Ritual*, he did not abolish any of the others. As far as can be discovered through research, those books remain acceptable for use even now. However, there are some issuances by the Vatican II, which remain hotly debated, that may indicate an abolishment of all previous books and a superseding of specific preexisting publications by newer or updated versions.

It is the most recent version of the *Roman Ritual*, published in 2008, that is referenced in this book regarding clerical actions, prayers, and conduct. The *Roman Ritual* does list specific preparatory steps necessary for a successful and less dangerous engagement with demonic forces. From this publication there are eight easily identified preparatory actions that the priest and others must take prior to opening an exorcism.[7] These steps are: imploring the divine for assistance; praying; fasting; encouraging others to pray for assistance; encouraging the afflicted person to pray; confessing, performing acts of contrition, and being absolved of sin; and studying the subject of possession and exorcism.

11.4.1.1 Imploring the Divine for Assistance

The priest, assigned as the clerical exorcist, and those who function as assistants must enter into deep and long-term prayer in order to acquire divine blessing, assistance, and protection throughout the process of exorcism. Being human, priests are as vulnerable to the darkness of evil as anyone else. It is not through the power of the individual priest but of the Holy Spirit that casts demons out. The priests are merely the vessels through which the power of God is channeled against the minions of Satan and his hell.

David most certainly would not have been able to defeat the likes of Goliath without the presence of God, the one and true divine being and

7. Weller, trans., *Roman Ritual*, 2:167, 169.

creator of all that is. It was indeed the will of God and the power of the Holy Spirit that gave courage to him, accuracy to the rock, and strength in the sling he gripped that day. Goliath, the personification of evil on earth at the time, most certainly would have made short work of David had David not been aided by the Lord, our God. So it is for the priest who goes forth to do combat with demons that have cruelly seized an innocent human body.

11.4.1.2 Prayer

In addition to the imploring for direct assistance from the divine, the priest must pray for the forgiveness of his or her own transgressions and sins. The priest must pray for the forgiveness of sins and for the body and soul of the afflicted person. The priest must pray that the possession subject will be delivered from the clutches of the Evil One. He or she must also pray for the success and protection of all others of this realm who step forward with him or her in warfare against the armies of hell.

Prayer is the most powerful tool in humanity's inventory of weapons against Lucifer and his subordinate demons. It is a spiritual outcry to the Lord God Almighty and his many angels. Prayer provides for a sword and shield that the demoniacal world is incapable of destroying. Prayer brings with it the light of the Holy Spirit, and through it come all that heaven has for the conquering of evil. One should never underestimate the power of prayer when preparing for battle with the elements of hell itself.

11.4.1.3 Fasting

Fasting was a sacrifice of self-denial practiced by Christians between the ages of sixteen and sixty even before Saint Peter entered Rome. It is essentially an adoption of a Jewish practice that predates the Lord Jesus Christ. This act is for the atonement of sin and not for strength of the Holy Spirit. Under the general term of *fasting*, there are at least three distinct forms of fasting practiced by Catholics around the world. In accordance with historical practice, there is *fasting* and *abstinence*.

Fasting is generally defined in church teachings as the reduction of food intake by the penitent to one full meal per twenty-four-hour day. This single meal is broken down into two eating sessions called *colla-*

tions. The first collation occurs early in the morning just before sunrise and the second occurs just after sunset, but the two combined make only the one full meal for the day. Consumption of water is permitted at anytime throughout the fast and in whatever quantity is desired by the penitent person. Still, for more radical Catholics, fasting allows only the consumption of water and no food intake at all. This type of fast is known as *absolute fasting.*

It is suspected that the absolute fast was what led to the eventual death of Anneliese Michel in 1976. Under these circumstances, she would have been allowed only minimal amounts of water and no other nutrient amounts whatsoever. The effects on her health were undoubtedly severe and do certainly match what is observed in available photographs of her near the last days of her life. The lack of much-needed nutrients also served to further the intensity and frequency of seizures and cause more frequent and intense episodes of psychosis. Whether or not fasting was the cause of her death, the facts, reported in the autopsy report, indicate that the cause of death was emaciation caused by malnutrition and dehydration. This is the most common condition encountered by people who practice dangerously long fasting of the absolute form.

The other form of fasting, known as abstinence, is further divided into complete and partial. Complete abstinence, practiced by individuals aged fourteen and older, involves the avoidance of meat while consuming other food items throughout the day. Partial abstinence allows for the consumption of meat one time each day and the consumption of other foods as usual. It is abstinence and not fasting that is most commonly practiced by Catholics during the season of Lent.

Fasting is, in all fact, an act of penance. It is a sacrifice that denies the body of food in order to achieve atonement for various sins committed by the fasting individual. Though many medieval Roman priests would quickly disagree this practice does not and has never before given the fasting individual any more or less power over the devil. This has placed this act, in regards to the afflicted person, in hot debate among demonologists and exorcists. Some argue that fasting is spiritually empowering while others counter with arguments of penance being penance and prayer being prayer. They further argue that fasting places the exorcism subject in unnecessary medical danger.

11.4.1.4 Encouraging Others to Pray for Assistance

Encouraging and directing others of the Christian faith to pray for strength and protection in regard to the afflicted person and themselves is an absolute necessity in a successful battle with the legions of the demonic realm. This is an activity that crosses through every form of Christian practice and faith. Prayer is humanity's most powerful weapon against evil and its many temptations. Those who ask for forgiveness and receive it are blessed by the hand of the Lord and are therefore strengthened against Satan (Ps 32:1–2).[8]

An common Catholic intersession practice is the use of the rosary (from Roman and Roman-related churches) and the chotki (for Eastern Orthodox churches). The rosary becomes an intercessory prayer activity when the mysteries are replaced with a single intercession prayer. At the first through fifth decade of the rosary,[9] a prayer is injected where normally the mystery would be recited. A common prayer used by both Roman and Orthodox Catholics when praying either the rosary or chotki is

> Lord Jesus Christ, son of the one true and living God, forgive
> ——'s sins and deliver him/her from the clutches of evil. Amen.

The chotki is a lesser-known Eastern Orthodox prayer tool that is most commonly seen as having either thirty or one hundred beads in a rope circle joined by a crucifix or the Jerusalem cross. Unlike the rosary of the Western Catholics, the chotki is a far more simple prayer method that has only two prayers to it. For some, the Nicene or Apostles' Creed is recited at the cross. Each bead represents one prayer of the following:

> Lord Jesus, son of the living God, forgive me, a sinner.

For many Roman exorcists, a special mass may be performed for the people close to the afflicted person and those who will be participating exorcism team members. This is also a very powerful and helpful preparatory activity. It allows the people to come together in requesting the Lord's assistance and the assistance of the saints, angels, and martyrs in heaven. It allows the faithful who will work to assist in the exorcism to be filled with the Holy Spirit and their sins washed away so as to be both protected and strengthened against evil.

8. All Bible references come from the New American Bible.
9. A "decade" consists of ten beads representing one Hail Mary Prayer each.

11.4.1.5 Encouraging the Afflicted Person to Pray

Any outcry to the Lord Jesus Christ and the Holy Father for salvation or deliverance from the forces of hell will be answered. The full wrath of heaven will rain down upon the evil specter that dares enter and torment the body, mind, and soul of the faithful (Acts 10:43). Therefore, if the afflicted person is not too tormented then he or she should be encouraged to recite the Lord's Prayer (Matt 6:9–13) and to participate in joint prayers of intercession through the rosary or chotki.

Accepting communion is another very powerful way to compel dark spirits to vacate the body of the faithful. This acceptance of the body and blood of Jesus Christ allows for the free pouring of the Holy Spirit into the invaded body and the removal of sin's stains upon the soul (Matt 26:28; Acts 13:38). The entry of the Holy Spirit and the removal of the sins through which the demon came will result in a more easily removed demonic entity.

11.4.1.6 Confession, Act of Contrition, and Absolution of Sin

Confession is the closest one may get, within Roman Christian practice, to a criminal confession. The difference is rather obvious in that the transgression is a violation of God's law and not those of people or governments. The person who is confessing is known as the *confessor*, and a priest hears and considers what is confessed. In more traditional Roman Catholic churches there is a special booth, called a *confessional*, where the priest and confessor meet in seclusion and privacy. However, the use of a confessional is not a requirement for confession to be heard.

The sacrament of Penance is the principle under which confession is both justified and encouraged for the faithful. The Roman tradition sees sin as a stain on the soul that must be washed away through a process of purification. The confessing of a sin and the subsequent act of penance given by the priest is seen as the means by which a sin's stains are removed from the souls of mankind. However, the Eastern Orthodox tradition sees things a bit differently in this regard.

In the many subgroups of the Eastern Orthodox Catholic faith, it is generally held that sin is not something which stains the soul but is nothing more than a mistake that requires correction. It is an act that requires rehabilitative assistance from the church and clergy and not something which forever haunts or defaces the inner soul of the person. Repentance is seen as an issue of individual spiritual development toward the grace and glory of the Lord God Almighty. Thus, a person learns from his or her mistakes to become a better Christian and to earn value in the eyes of God. A person is deprived of God through sin and not condemned outright.

There are many split-off Catholic churches of Roman origin or basis whose perspective on and practice of confession are quite similar if not identical. For the New American Catholic Church (NACC), a relatively new addition to the splinter Roman churches, the practice of confession is remarkably similar to that practiced by the traditional Roman Church. The process for the NACC is:

A. Preconfession. The confessor must first recognize his or her sin and be truly and completely remorseful for the deed. He or she usually makes a list of all sins on a piece of paper to be taken into the confessional so that nothing is forgotten.

B. Confession.
   1. The confessor, after making the sign of the cross, declaring how long it had been since last confession, and listening to the reading of selected scripture by the priest, then confesses completely and truthfully all sins. The priest will listen intently and may ask questions for clarification or offer comments of advice or spiritual encouragement.
   2. After stating his or her last sin, the confessor recites the Act of Contrition. This is a special prayer that expresses sorrow for the sin, the pain caused to God, the remorse felt, and the determination to never repeat the sin.
   3. The priest will advise the confessor on the penance to be performed in order to make good for the sin committed. When the penance has completed, the absolution will prevail. If it is ignored, then the sin remains.

C. Absolution. Absolution is given through a special prayer that forgives the sinner and absolves him or her of judgment. This is, of course, dependent upon the completion of the penance proscribed.

For the Catholic priest, it is critical that he go through the process of confession, include all transgressions of deed and thought, pray the Act of Contrition, and receive absolution from another priest before engaging in an exorcism.[10] At the very least, he should pray the Act of Contrition before performing an exorcism session.

11.4.1.6 Intense Study on the Subject of Possession and Exorcism

The Roman rite stresses the importance of studying and being as academically familiar with the subject and condition of demonic possession as possible. It encourages the reading of books and theses written by approved authors and on acquiring the advice of experienced exorcists elsewhere in the clerical community of the church.

There is no doubting that intense study and the seeking of advice from more experienced exorcists is necessary in order for the assigned priest to become fully aware of and prepared for an exorcism battle with the elements of hell. That being said, there are a few warnings that should be heeded in this regard. One should not be to ready to believe everything written by a church-approved author on the subject of exorcism.

Beware of exaggeration and outright fabrication of information regarding actual and alleged possession cases and working of wondrous deeds on the part of the author or any featured exorcist. For instance, William Blatty, a skilled and successful writer of Lebanese origin, wrote the novel entitled, *The Exorcist*. The story is only loosely based on an actual exorcism case reported to have occurred in 1949 and consists of what many believe to be creative inserts for enhancing the entertainment value of the story. Dr. M. Scott Peck, a psychiatrist and exorcist wrote, "*The Exorcist* was a very good read on those stormy nights, but it was in no way believable by the light of day."[11] A work of fiction solely intended to entertain the masses should not, under any circumstances, be read as an actual case history of demonic possession.

One must also be very objective and realistic in the readings and lectures of others who proclaim to have performed actual exorcisms or gained special knowledge of the demonic realm. This author believes that the likes of Malachi Martin, author of *Hostage to the Devil*, should be taken with a grain of salt. In regards to Malachi Martin, Dr. Peck writes, "Indeed, he was perhaps the most bald-faced liar I have ever known." Dr. Martin wrote a book about five exorcisms performed in America as if he were the actual exorcist. But, when directly asked about this, he always

---

10. Weller, trans., *Roman Ritual*, 2:167.
11. Peck, *Glimpses of the Devil*, 2.

evaded answering either in the affirmative or negative.[12] The inquiring party should see warning signs regarding the authenticity and credibility of what is being reported in cases where the alleged expert intentionally avoids answering simple and direct questions or has written incredibly dramatic and fairy-tale-like descriptions.

11.4.2 Protestant

Protestant Christendom is a very complex web of faiths and splinter faiths. Some have an idea of deliverance and others do not address the subject of demonic influence at all. There are a plethora of books and even theses written by various ministers of various faiths but no standard concept to follow in regards to demonic warfare. What is worse is that the information one minister of one Protestant faith writes and shares is argued and rejected by ministers of other Protestant faiths. Fragmentation and heated disagreement by and between these churches makes the creation of a standardized text and procedure near impossible.

11.4.2.1 Prayer

Prayer is present in every element of Christendom. It is humanity's most powerful tool for combating and preventing the infestation of evil and willful sin by the faithful. The minister is compelled to pray for strength from God through the Holy Spirit and spends time confessing to the Lord and receiving forgiveness so as to be strengthened against the works of the devil. The minister prays for the afflicted and those affected by the afflicted.

The minister will often pray with the person who is suspected of being demonically afflicted. The most common prayer is that of the Lord's Prayer found in the Book of Mathew 6:9–13. Scripture readings from the Book of Psalms and the Gospels are also used in joint sessions of prayer and worship designed to receive forgiveness from sin and deliverance from evil.

12. Peck, *Glimpses of the Devil*, 5.

11.4.2.2 Encouraging Others to Pray

In addition to individual and joint prayer with the afflicted by the minister, it is also important for close friends, family, and members of the faith to join in prayer. Praying in a group for the deliverance of the afflicted is a powerful spiritual approach to the process of ridding a person of his or her demons. It is equally important as a preparatory activity in order to cleanse and strengthen the supporting faithful as they join in the confrontation of the demoniacal world under the leadership of the church reverend.

Appropriate preparation is essential to success in determining and performing an exorcism. If one is dealing with a true possession, then being spiritually pure and strengthened is essential for the exorcist's mere survival. The afflicted person must also be protected through physical and spiritual preparation. A lack of careful consideration for every element of preparation, as is provided in this chapter, could lead to a disaster.

12

Execution of the Rite

REGARDLESS OF WHICH EXORCISM or deliverance ritual is implemented to help a person suspected of being demonically possessed, it is critical that the ritual be reviewed to identify all potential elements that might generate unsafe conditions. It is strongly suggested to remove, or not perform, those elements of a particular ritual that may be archaic. There is absolutely no gain in a battle with the demonic where the physical body, the temple of the individual soul, is destroyed in the process.

The priest, minister, or other form of exorcist should have the full authority to skip those aspects or elements of a particular ritual that may be more likely to cause harm to the subject or others than to provide any form of comfort or help. The exorcist must always remember that he or she is liable under the laws of God and humanity for the harmful consequences of an exorcism session. Indeed, the Bible does say that a person who has accepted the Holy Spirit and remains in absolute faith to the Lord our God shall be empowered with the ability to drive out demonic entities. But, this power comes from the glorious compassion of the Lord and one must, in turn, show compassion, care, and mercy for the afflicted who has asked for help.

12.1 SAFETY CONCERNS AND MAINTENANCE

Safety for both the physical and spiritual well-being of the subject and the exorcism team should always be foremost on the mind of the exorcist. It should also be foremost on the minds of each member of the team. Every member of the team has a responsibility and obligation to be on the lookout for anything that may present a danger, in any form, to the subject of the exorcism or any participant or observer of the exorcism.

The site of the exorcism should be well reviewed and modified as needed to ensure an environment as safe as is absolutely possible for the afflicted and the members of the exorcism team. The use of restraints of any form is strongly discouraged as they really aren't needed. Fellow members of the team can intercept and cease any attack made by the subject during session-related rages or outbursts. The use of a space that restricts maneuverability should not occur. The space selected should be large enough to allow all participants to maneuver in order to evade impact with flying objects and physical assaults by the afflicted individual. Even the installation of floor and wall padding is recommended so as to greatly reduce the likelihood of injury to anyone participating in or observing the exorcism or deliverance service.

All furniture and wall decorations should be removed from the exorcism chamber so as to enhance the safety of the environment. It is strongly recommended that no chairs or even a bed be in the chamber. The afflicted may sit or lay upon the padded floor throughout the exorcism session and the team members may be seated on the padded floor as well. They can stand if that is so elected.

Additionally, nothing sharp should be brought into the room. Medical supplies should be maintained just outside of the room and guarded by a medical professional. This keeps instruments and needles away from a potentially violent person while maintaining sufficient proximity for a quick medical response in a crisis or emergency. Car keys, cell phones, purses, or anything else that may be used by the afflicted or other person to cause harm to someone should not be brought into the room.

Above all, every person participating in or observing the exorcism or deliverance session has the obligation to their fellow humans and the requirement under the laws and teachings of the Lord Jesus Christ to bring attention to anything that may be immoral, unlawful, dangerous, or in any other way harmful to anyone. Each and every person in the exorcism team, as well as those who may simply be observing the exorcism, has the legal and moral responsibility to stop, or act to stop, any action or lack of action that appears to be negatively affecting the health or safety of the exorcism subject or other person. Even if the others, present and participating, disagree and encourage continuance without rendering aid, the doubting individual is obligated under the Christian teachings of love, compassion, and mercy for others to act in the interests of the affected person's safety.

The Anneliese Michel exorcism case is a perfect example of the abandonment of compassion, love, and mercy by the participants of an exorcism. Such actions led to the untimely and unnecessary loss of the young girl's life. What divine judgment should we expect for those responsible for watching the young Anneliese waste away into the darkness of death through the conduct of over sixty individual exorcism sessions?

Common sense should also prevail in regard to safety. If, as in the Klingenberg case, sixty or so exorcism ritual sessions have not lessened the individual's suffering or experiences, then common sense should come into play and prompt the exorcist and others related to the exorcism to consider the fact that the person may not actually be afflicted with demons but rather with some mental or physical illness. The Bible gives us several examples of exorcism. Many are conducted by the Lord Jesus Christ himself. Not one of these sessions lasted for months or even weeks for Christ, the apostles, or the seventy disciples. It is wise to follow the example of Scripture and reevaluate the situation when nothing is achieved at the conclusion of the fourth exorcism or deliverance session.

12.2 CONSTANT MEDICAL MONITORING

In order to ensure that the safety and well-being for the exorcism subject is maintained, it is essential that the medical element of the exorcism team perform constant monitoring of vital signs and other conditions, as necessary, throughout each exorcism or deliverance service. The use of EKG, EEG, and other electronic instruments in addition to more traditional blood pressure measuring and other devices is strongly encouraged where and when available. But, at the very least, the medical team member should measure the blood pressure, pulse, and temperature of the subject in addition to other examinations throughout the session and for a time immediately following the conclusion of a session. Blood sugar should be checked frequently for subjects diagnosed with diabetes even when the subject does not take insulin injections.

Dehydration is a serious threat to the subject during an exorcism. This is especially so when the session is lengthy (greater than two hours). Thus, the medical team members should not only observe the subject for signs of dehydration and heat exhaustion but ensure that the subject is consuming water on a regular frequency and at an adequate volume to prevent dehydration. Water consumption by the other members of the exorcism team must also be monitored and encouraged in order to prevent dehydration.

The medical team element is also chiefly responsible for ensuring that the medical condition of the subject and other team members remain adequately capable of enduring the ordeals and stresses involved in the process of exorcism or deliverance. Had the exorcists in the Anneliese Michel exorcism been more attentive, even slightly, to Anneliese's medical condition and physical needs, then she would have survived the ordeal. Unfortunately, this wasn't the case, and the young girl died as a result of neglect through misguided faith.

Regardless, the primary concern of the medical team element is to ensure safety for the subject of the exorcism and the other members of the exorcism team. Not only have medical professionals sworn to render aid when it is needed but they are also legally obligated to render aid to or find aid for those in desperate need of it. Indeed, all people are so obligated to their fellows as to ensure assistance where assistance is needed to prevent serious harm or death. It should be completely understood by the leading exorcist and by the religious supporters of the exorcism team that the medical element may, at any time it deems necessary, call a halt to the entire exorcism or deliverance process and render aid, stabilize, or call aid for any person who, in the professional's opinion, is in need of immediate medical attention.

12.3 CONDUCTING THE RITE AS REQUIRED BY FAITH

Each Christian faith form, or denomination, has its own procedures and practices regarding the removal of evil spirits from the body of human beings or to remove human beings from their influences. Many of these procedures and rituals were written by pious and well-intended spiritual academics many hundreds of years ago, and others were more recent in their development. Some efforts are created during a minister's confrontation with the demonic realm itself in a sort of combative ad-lib scenario.

It is important that the procedures of the particular faith facing the demonic entity be followed as closely as possible. However, those procedures that have existed for more than one hundred years without review or revision should be followed with an air of caution. It is important to always remember that what was defined with less information one hundred years or more ago may indeed be better understood today. Where common sense and the moral obligations proscribed by God and God's Holy Son, Jesus Christ, indicate that a part of an archaic practice should be abandoned or modified, then it should be. We are creatures who are self-aware and know the difference between what is right and what is wrong (Gen 3:22) and therefore are held responsible for allowing what is wrong, knowing it to be wrong or inaccurate at the time of its doing, to perpetuate further. This is especially so where wrongful practice or practice based on wrongful thinking has the potential to result in a serious injury or the death of the afflicted person or any other person participating in the ritual.

It must be remembered that science is not a blasphemy to Christendom or the Lord our God. It is a process of discovery that further defines the laws God made. It is a spiritual evolution as well as an academic one. Scientists simply unveil what was happening around the cosmos since its creation by the divine so many millions of years ago. They, the scientists, are not the enemy of God but rather God's students in the physical realm. These, our brothers and sisters, have discovered what exists by the will of God, how that which exists works by the will of God, and they discover how what exists interacts with other things that exist by the will of God. They use what God made via the laws God enacted to create new things and these, being created by humans, are not as perfect as that made by God. If what was practiced hundreds of years ago is today proven to be erroneous, then it should be modified to be correct or abandoned in favor of what is correct.

Faith is the belief in the one true and living God, his Holy Son, Jesus Christ, and the power of the Holy Spirit. Faith is the belief that our Holy Savior, the Lord Jesus Christ, was tortured and died in order that we may be forgiven in our sinful states and redeemed in heaven. Faith is the belief that adherence to the laws of God, maker of all that is and will be, and the teachings of the most Holy Christ will deliver us, one and all, from the clutches of the Evil One. Faith is not the belief or indulgence of human-made traditions and rules that may or do cause harm to others.

12.4 CONTINUOUS DOCUMENTATION OF EVENTS

Throughout the entire process of investigation, determination, review of conclusions, the performance of the exorcism and all follow-ups to the exorcism must be documented both in written and audiovisual records. Nothing should be left out or overlooked in documenting the events that take place, the actions taken by all involved, and the experiences of each and all members of the exorcism team. Such documentation is necessary for many reasons.

One reason for continuous documentation is to provide for a thorough history of events for use by future generations in study and application of the practice. How is one to teach and another to learn without records to reference? Another reason is so that questions of due diligence and accusations of negligence may be thoroughly answered for any given exorcism event. How is one to prove that due diligence and regard occurred without records? How is one to prove that no negligent conduct occurred without event records?

Ensuring that safety is maintained, medical monitoring is constant and available, and that the rules established by the faith are adhered to will allow for a successful expulsion of demonic entities from the body of the innocent. Properly and completely documenting the history of events and conditions encountered will allow for future learning and understanding regarding the activities and methods of demonic entities. Additionally, there are potential legal matters that may be positively addressed and overcome through the evidence provided in a well-documented activity.

PART 5

Ethical, Moral, and Legal Issues

A right rule of conduct must be one which may with advantage
be adopted by all.

—Herbert Spencer, 1879

13

Ethics in Practice

ONE OF THE DEFINITIVE elements of a truly professional practice is the existence of a code of ethics that are accepted, followed, and enforced by all who are in that field. Throughout the many years, exorcists have existed in varying numbers but have gone without written standards of conduct and professional practice. There may have been a code of ethics created by the secretive Roman Demonology Club, known as the International Association of Exorcists and created by one of the Vatican's many dinosaur priests, like Frather Gabriel Amorth, during the eighties. But, since they choose to remain secret and perpetuate the ignorance of the faithful we must only speculate as to such a standard's actual existence.

It is absolutely vital that all of those people that choose to enter into spiritual combat with the devil and his minions be aware of and held to high standards of conduct and practice in order to ensure the success of exorcisms or deliverances and to ensure the safety of those who come to them for help. The absence of standards and the absence of due regard through misguided faith, hysterical states, and lack of training has been the chief culprit in deaths and serious injuries resulting from haphazard and botched exorcism practices.

13.1 AVOIDING PERSONAL GAIN

One cannot serve God and fortune at the same time (Matt 6:24). You are either in service of the holy order of the Lord God, creator of all that was, is, and will be, or you are a servant to greed and the attainment of fame and fortune. Never can a person be servant to both money and God.

Any person who performs or participates in an exorcism with the intention of making a profit from it is not in the proper moral and spiritual mindset. It is said in the holy Gospels that the devil cannot cast himself out (Matt 12:24–28). If it is fame and fortune that fills the mind and heart of the exorcist or any person participating in an exorcism then there can be no success in driving out the entity, as the stain of greed smears the souls of the ill intentioned. Greed is a great sin, and profiting upon the misfortune and suffering of another affronts the Lord our God.

13.2 AVOIDING PUBLICIZING THE EXORCISM

Self-aggrandizement is a lethal sin, as its origin is pride. The person stained with the sin of pride is one who cannot drive out demons but instead has become like one of them. To boast of having triumphed over evil as if it were one's own power that achieved it is to blaspheme through arrogance, for it is not the power of the exorcist but that of the Lord God, maker of all that is, that drives them out.

To make a show of an exorcism or deliverance is to cast the afflicted person, who came under your shelter for protection, into the hands of the ridiculing and evil crowds of Sodom and Gomorrah! It subjects the person and family to undue humiliation and suffering by the crowds. This suffering becomes the sin of the advertising and self-promoting exorcist. An exorcist cannot drive out demons in such a condition as this, as the exorcist has become like one of them.

Therefore, be pure of heart and seek to protect the afflicted demoniac and his or her family. Do not boast and do not advertise what is taking place, but act discretely. Do not publish written works that expose the subject or others to public identification and humiliation. Do not speak of them or any other matter related to the exorcism or deliverance in a public forum or with strangers in your midst. Do not hand the innocent over to be devoured by the evil hordes.

13.3 MAINTAINING THE CONFIDENTIALITY STANDARD

The exorcist, exorcism-supervising organization or religious order, and the individual members of the exorcism team are bound to protect the confidentiality of the exorcism subject and all other people involved, directly and indirectly, with the exorcism process. It should be agreed, preferably in an enforceable written agreement, that each participant will not divulge the personal information, including the name, of any of the other participants without their express written consent.

There are elements of every society who will seek to exploit people who have been involved in exorcisms, mainly through sensationalist news reporting and haphazard documentaries. There are others who will seek to purposefully degrade and ridicule the exorcism subject and all who helped him or her for no other reason than to cause emotional harm. The exorcists and entire exorcism team must strive to protect the subject and themselves from such senseless harassment and branding by those more influenced by the devil than they may be aware.

The concept of confidentiality is not intended to prohibit any person from notifying authorities or emergency services where such help is deemed necessary by the individual. It does not and should never be taken to mean that a person is prohibited from independently reporting any act, failure to act, or condition that is unsafe, immoral, un-Christian, or illegal to appropriate authorities. Confidentiality is restricted to the sharing of personal information and does not mean that a person should remain silent when an immoral or illegal act, omission, or condition is witnessed or observed.

In the Anneliese Michel exorcism case, secrecy was demanded and strictly enforced to such an extent that the young lady withered and died without a single person having called for medical assistance in the matter. It is mind-boggling for many to see or hear of others who have taken confidentiality to mean silence about the matter even when someone is in danger of being killed. But, it has happened many times over the years, with the latest one having occurred in 2005 involving an Eastern Orthodox Catholic nun named Sister Maricica; this tragedy will be discussed later in chapter 15.

13.4 AVOIDING EXPLOITATION

Following the conclusion of the very well-publicized trial of Father Alt, Father Renz, and Anneliese's parents that started in 1978, some of the involved parties went about the business of conducting paid lectures, interviews, documentary spots, and written works on the subject. It is unimportant to mention these persons here; the point is that money-making became a priority immediately following the criminal trial when details could be discussed without the testimony being used against individuals in court.

The physicians remained silent and followed their ethical code regarding the confidentiality of their patient. They remained professional throughout Anneliese's ordeal and beyond. Unfortunately, others involved in the incident went skipping out the courtroom doors with the proverbial thirty pieces of silver jingling in their pockets. In this author's opinion, these people spoke with every TV show producer, documentary producer, magazine, and book publisher available in order to tell the story of Klingenberg's demon.

One should never exploit the loss or suffering of another in order to achieve fame or fortune. This also falls under the deadly sins of greed and pride. The Klingenberg case has been built up to be some sort of holy war fought in a home with the unfortunate loss of the possession victim. Much of this exaggeration has been created and promoted by exploitive participants in the incident. Those who gleefully line their pockets with silver and gold at the expense of one who has suffered greatly are among the lowest of the low in the eyes of God. This is especially so for those who are responsible for the suffering of the person they exploit.

13.5 MAINTAINING THOROUGHNESS IN INVESTIGATION

No matter what is being explored or investigated, detail and thoroughness are essential in gaining a full and complete understanding of the subject. The same is so in regard to the investigation of suspected demonic activity. The professional and competent exorcist or demonologist will leave no stone unturned, no lead unfollowed, and no hunch un-indulged.

13.6 PROMOTING THE EMOTIONAL AND PSYCHOLOGICAL WELL-BEING OF THE VICTIM

It is the goal of the exorcist and the entire exorcism team to free the subject from the grip and influence of satanic forces. In achieving this goal, every effort should be made to preserve and ensure the emotional and psychological well-being of the subject. It is the responsibility of the exorcist and the entire exorcism team to act, or not act, in every matter and in such a manner as to not jeopardize, harm, or worsen the subject's emotional and physical condition.

13.7 RESPECTING THE STANDARD OF PHYSICAL SAFETY FOR ALL PERSONNEL

The condition of Ms. Anneliese Michel's body at the time of her death revealed numerous bruises upon her face, wrists, hands, and other parts of her body. Several of the defendants claimed, during the 1978 criminal trial, that the young girl inflicted the wounds on herself. This may have been the case, but two issues arise from this. First, the environment in which the exorcism sessions took place was not made safe enough. Second, the exorcists, upon seeing that the girl was harming herself, failed to take appropriate action to prevent her from inflicting the injuries or, at the very least, to halt the sessions entirely until more safe conditions could be arranged.

The professional exorcist or demonologist is responsible for any injuries sustained by any participant in an exorcism session regardless of how those injuries are caused. Every effort must be made by the exorcist and the members of the exorcism team to mitigate dangers to personnel and onlookers. The exorcist must cease all exorcism or deliverance activities when conditions deteriorate to a point where injury, even in the most minor of forms, is sustained by the subject or any other person involved in the exorcism session.

13.8 PROMOTING THE TRUTH IN REPORTING AND FULL DISCLOSURE OF EVIDENCE

The thorough collection and examination of data and evidence is critical in determining whether a person is suffering from mental illness, executing a fraud, or genuinely possessed by demons. The amount and quality of the evidence, to include credibility, is critical in justifying the performance of any exorcism or deliverance ritual. Every exorcist is bound to report truthfully, accurately, and completely on all details, matters, and events related to a suspected case of demonic possession or any actual case of demonic possession.

It is unethical for any exorcist, minister, priest, or demonologist to present facts in a misleading manner, to omit facts in order to lean the case toward a preferred conclusion, or to fabricate facts in order to achieve some personal or organizational goal. Doing so not only destroys the individual's credibility but may also result in harm to the subject of investigation and any subsequent exorcism or deliverance service.

13.9 MAINTAINING THE INTEGRITY STANDARD FOR INVESTIGATORS AND EXORCISTS

No one believes a liar and no one trusts a deceiver. It only takes one incident of willful deceit or fabrication of truth for a person to forever be branded a liar or cheat. An entire church community or organization can suffer tremendous damage to its reputation through the deceitful actions of a single person. Regardless of one's wealth, a person has nothing without integrity.

Additionally, the legal consequences for the exorcist, minister, priest, demonologist, or participating team member can be overwhelming when deceit is used to justify an exorcism that later results in serious harm or death to the subject of the exorcism. Such actions can be used by prosecuting attorneys as evidence of malice aforethought and the presence of a malignant heart. Litigating attorneys can also use a lack of integrity or deceitful reporting against a defendant in a wrongful death lawsuit. If a person is proven to be a liar, then how is any jury expected to believe what that person says?

Aside from the legal ramifications, there are also professional consequences for a person who has been exposed as a fraud, liar, or other form of deceiver. No other member of the demonological, spiritual, or Christian communities will even consider the theories, reports, and arguments made by a person who lacks integrity or is deceitful in any way.

13.10 MAINTAINING OBJECTIVITY

The professional demonologist or exorcist remains objective throughout all aspects of the exorcism process. He or she does not allow personal bias and emotions to dictate his or her perspective under any circumstances. Data is collected and observations are recorded in their raw and real form without personal bias or belief spin. No report or item of evidence should be scripted or presented in a manner that misrepresents or causes an understanding other than what actually is.

14

Civil Law and the Practice

B EFORE DELVING INTO THE various civil torts that may apply to the practice of exorcisms, it is important to fully understand the differences between civil and criminal codes and the ramifications of each. While there are many instances where the two codes overlap in theory, they are separate and apart from one another. A person cannot be tried in the two separate arenas at the same time for the same offense, or perceived offense. That being said, a person may be tried in criminal court with a civil suit to follow under certain situations.

In its simplest form, civil law is defined as all noncriminal laws. There are of course many subcategories found under the auspices of that definition, but essentially, violations of civil law will not result in incarceration of any form. The ramifications are monetary and often substantial. Make no mistake, civil litigation can be just as stressful as a criminal trial, but individual freedoms are not at stake.

It may seem strange to many that any consideration of noncriminal proceedings would be mentioned in a work dealing with the rites and rituals of exorcism. On the contrary, any person undertaking such activity must always keep in mind the hazard of civil liability. Remember, this is noncriminal prosecution. These proceedings do not require any type of law enforcement investigation for a suit to be brought to trial. Any person at any time can file a civil lawsuit for any reason regardless of the validity of the claim.

Therefore, any person who conducts activities such as exorcisms must always be mindful of the risk of civil litigation and liability. Failure to fully understand those risks and taking proactive steps to mitigate them will result in catastrophic consequences.

14.1 WRONGFUL DEATH

The concept of wrongful death took hold in the United States during the westward expansion period of the 1800s. During that time, workers for the railroad began filing suits against employers for injuries sustained on the job. In *Farwell v. Boston & Worcester Railway* (1842), the Massachusetts Supreme Court upheld the employer's rights, stating that the employees had to prove negligent actions on the part of the employer. The court determined that the job held inherent risks, and it was the responsibility of the workers to not only know the risks involved but to mitigate them regardless of circumstance. This ruling held steadfast for more than fifty years, making it virtually impossible for an employee to successfully litigate against an employer for injuries sustained on the job.[1]

As injuries and deaths caused by the construction of the railroad continued to mount, Congress began to feel the pressure to act. The Federal Employers Liability Act of 1908 was a direct result of this force. For the first time in U.S. history, employers of the railroad were held fiscally liable for the injuries as well as the deaths that occurred while working. The Merchant Maritime Act of 1920 followed and incorporated the same level of employer liability to seafaring occupations.

Over time it became quite clear that, although these laws were good, they did not cover the various circumstances that could result in death or injury. Since that time, each state has enacted separate laws to incorporate individual acts of negligence and harm that may result in the death of another individual. While these laws vary from state to state, they essentially incorporate the same language. Any person who commits a wanton or wrongful act that results in the death of another individual or groups of individuals will be held civilly liable for that death. This includes negligent behavior, which can be achieved through either action or inaction depending on the circumstances.

1. John Fabian Witt, "Federal Employers Liability Act," Enotes.com, http://www.enotes.com/major-acts-congress/federal-employers-liability-act.

How would such a statute apply to the case of Anneliese Michel? In this particular instance, the priest and the parents had full control over the living conditions of a person who was no longer deemed capable of everyday functions. They were responsible for making sure that she received the necessary food to sustain life, which clearly did not happen. They were also responsible for ensuring that she did not receive injury, and that also didn't happen. According to the testimony of the coroner, there were numerous bruises and injuries around her body. Through the direct actions of each of the members, or the lack of actions on their part, Anneliese Michel lost her life. Could this have been a wrongful death lawsuit based on that fact? Absolutely! Why wasn't this case brought up in civil litigation? The answer is quite simply that there wasn't anyone to bring this type of case up at the time. Most statutes require that the immediate family bring the suit to court. In this case, that would have been the parents, who received a conviction in criminal court.

Obviously, there is no way to bring the spiritual realm into the court of law. An exorcised demon, no matter how confined, will not show up under subpoena to testify on the behalf of the exorcist as to the extent of the possession. Therefore extreme caution must be utilized to mitigate liability of such a suit. Those who rush into the fray in the hopes of a publishable manuscript later run the risk of a dangerous potential of lawsuit, especially in the event of a death.

14.2 NEGLIGENCE RESULTING IN PHYSICAL OR MENTAL INJURIES

The negligence statute follows the same lines as the wrongful death claim and can trace its history through the same initial legislative evolution. Under this legal concept, the actions caused injury but fell short of death. These suits may be brought by the individual, or, in cases where incapacitation has occurred, by immediate family members.

In one application of this legal concept, the victim must prove that the defendant held a duty to care for the victim and that a reasonable person would have been able to determine that the actions, or lack of actions, in question would result in harm. The question in this regard is whether there is a duty to render aid to a person in need of aid or if the plaintiff was dependent upon the defendant for care and the defendant acted or failed to act in accordance with those duties in such a way that the direct result was serious injury to the plaintiff.

In similarity to wrongful death suits, judgment varies based on the laws of each state, the severity of the injury, and duration of the activity. Laws generally allow for individuals to claim loss of wages, medical bills, and living expenses as well as compensation for pain, suffering, humiliation, and overall distress. It is very possible for the amounts to top the million dollar mark relatively quickly.

14.3: MITIGATING CIVIL LIABILITY

Understanding the risks associated with the rites of exorcism is important but fruitless without considerations for mitigating those risks. While one may never be able to fully remove the fiscal concerns, one can certainly take actions to avoid unnecessary legal actions.

First and foremost, due diligence must be used at all times during all phases of the ritual. Improper documentation, omitting evaluation steps, failing to seek out medical experts, and relying heavily on the unseen are litigation traps. If you cannot articulate each of the actions taken throughout the entire process with supportive documentation, there is a very real chance that you would lose a civil case if filed.

There are those in the profession who still practice such tactics but have crafted liability release statements. A release of liability will not protect against negligence. There is no release waiver that can protect against negligence, no matter how well crafted. This sheet of paper is nothing more than a false sense of security. It will not protect an individual performing the rites of exorcism who fails to use due diligence in the performance of those duties.

15

Criminal Law and the Practice

THIS CHAPTER IS INTENDED to render examples of possible and probable criminal consequences for negligence in the performance of exorcism and for the execution of any wanton or knowingly reckless act. It is not asserted as legal advice in any way, and the reader is encouraged to conduct independent legal research and to seek the advice and assistance of a properly licensed and trained legal professional before moving forward with the performance of an exorcism.

This chapter does serve a great purpose for the ministerial and demonological community, however. Where exorcism is undertaken without proper consideration for safety and legality, a practitioner assumes a tremendous and unnecessary moral, legal, and spiritual risk. This chapter focuses on the possible legal consequences of negligence or improperly performed exorcism or deliverance services. The most important information to remember from this chapter is that churches, ministers, bishops, priests, theologians, and demonologists are not immune from criminal prosecution for deaths or serious injuries that result from religious or spiritual practices and traditions.

15.1 NEGLIGENT HOMICIDE

Negligent homicide, more commonly known as manslaughter, is the criminal charge that is most frequently seen against exorcists and exorcism participants around the world. This was the sole charge prosecuted against Father Ernst Alt, Father Arnold Renz, Josef Michel, and Anna Michel in the Anneliese Michel exorcism case. The more recent 2005 case of Sister Maricica's exorcism fatality in Romania also resulted in the conviction of one orthodox priest and four nuns of manslaughter.

Manslaughter is most commonly defined as the unlawful killing of a human being without malice or premeditation, either express or implied. It is also divided into five classifications in order to allow for specific handling of and sentencing for particular manslaughter behavior or circumstance. These classifications are: (1) provocation, (2) mutual combat, (3) resistance to public officials acting unlawfully, (4) killing in prosecution of an unlawful or wanton act, and (5) killing in the execution of a lawful act, or improperly performed lawful act, or without lawful authorization.

The fifth classification of manslaughter is of most concern to exorcists and those who assist them or participate in exorcism rituals. Most statutes and prosecutors see no difference in what some call a deliverance service and others call an exorcism. If a minister misapplies a ritual, invents a ritual that a reasonable person would recognize as dangerous or negligent, or does anything that is definable and recognizable as negligent or reckless and a death results, then the minister, along with others present and participating, may be subject to arrest, prosecution, and imprisonment for manslaughter.

In 1960, an appellate case heard in the Second District Court of Appeals, Division 3, of the State of California reviewed the case of the *People v. Rodriguez*. The defendant in the case had been convicted of involuntary manslaughter after her two-year-old child died in a home fire to which she did not respond appropriately when initial cries for help were heard.[1] A neighbor from across the street responded and helped evacuate the other three children but could not rescue the fourth and youngest child. Because the mother was inebriated, and did not exhibit sound judgment in recognizing the risk she posed to her children should an emergency occur, the appeal was denied. The defendant was found to be negligent, even though it was lawful to drink alcohol.

The result of the aforementioned case was the generally accepted ruling and confirmation that an act of negligence is definable as any act, lawful or unlawful, that a prudent person would foresee as causing a high degree of risk for death or serious bodily injury. The ruling court

1. *People v. Rodriguez*, 186 Cal. App. 2d 433 and 8 Cal. Rptr. 863, 1960.

held that the risk of death or serious bodily injury must be great in order to constitute criminal negligence sufficient to sustain a conviction of involuntary manslaughter.

In *People v. Penny*, the defendant was convicted of involuntary manslaughter after a customer died during a skin rejuvenation treatment.[2] The compound used contained phenol, and the defendant, while mixing the formula, used an excessive amount of phenol. The cause of death was determined as phenol poisoning. The appeal was based on the lack of criminal negligence in the case and a request for the overturning of the conviction was asserted. However, the appellate court upheld the conviction on the grounds that due caution and circumspection was not exercised by the defendant, which later resulted in the death of the victim.

The result of *People v. Penny* is that "knowledge, actual or imputed, that the act of the slayer tended to endanger life and that the fatal consequences could have been foreseen are necessary for negligence to be criminal at all." It may seem to be a bit of a stretch between tragic fire, lethal facials, and exorcism-related death. But, it is far from it, as the same rule applied to the two aforementioned cases is applied to every case of manslaughter, involuntary and voluntary.

If the prosecution can show that the performance of an exorcism included a willful disregard for safety or life-threatening probabilities that a reasonable person would have identified and foreseen, then an exorcist, and many of the participating parties, could certainly find themselves charged and convicted of involuntary manslaughter. This is why it is of utmost concern to all persons involved in an exorcism or deliverance ritual to take steps towards the elimination of bodily risks for the subject and all participants of such activity. This is also why it is important that the exorcist, and every member of the exorcism team, remain diligent in looking for and recognizing potential and actual dangers before they manifest into a serious bodily injury or death. There must be obvious and documented evidence that every reasonable step towards assuring safety and reducing risks have been taken to, first, ensure the safety and well-being of human life and, second, reduce criminal liability in the event that charges are filed. Regardless, protecting and preserving human life and mental well-being should always be foremost on everyone's mind.

2. 44 Cal.2d 861 and 285 P.2d 926.

15.2 MURDER (FIRST AND SECOND DEGREE)

In many reported cases of death resulting from exorcism or deliverance services, the exorcist is originally arrested and charged with murder. Through the legal process, this charge is usually reduced to manslaughter as a condition to a plea agreement or through legal argument before magistrates and higher-level judges. At least one case included a judge allowing a jury to convict on the lesser charge of manslaughter described in section 15.1 above. However, as the frequency of exorcism-induced homicide continues to rise, one should expect law enforcement and prosecuting authorities to become less inclined to allow criminal reductions in the future.

15.2.1 First-Degree Murder

There are three basic elements to the crime of first-degree murder. In order to be convicted of this capital offense, one must first kill another human being, second have malice aforethought, and third premeditate the lethal act. This crime is often a capital offense that can carry a sentence of death or life imprisonment without possibility of parole. The possibility of a conviction being achieved against a minister or other exorcist for first-degree murder, in regards to a death that resulted from an exorcism, is exceptionally slim.

Although the possibility of a first-degree murder conviction is generally seen as slim, there are prosecutors and law enforcers, hare-brained as they may be, who would certainly assert arguments, depending on the wording of the applicable statutes, that a death caused by or during an exorcism ritual was first-degree murder. These individuals assert that the actions in preparation of the exorcism or deliverance ritual, which include finding a place for performance, ritual items, and holy water, constitutes premeditation. They would also say that the exorcist knew that the ritual was capable of resulting in human death and, in performing the rite, acted in a way that illustrated a complete disregard for human life and the knowledge that he or she would be killing another human being. Of course, the dead person is all that is needed to show that another human being was killed.

The preceding is certainly a stretch of law and legal interpretation. But, it is a real possibility in view of the fact that several prosecutors and investigators, interviewed throughout the United States, indicated that they would try to push a first-degree murder conviction against any person, minister or otherwise, whose exorcism or deliverance ritual resulted in the death of a person. This certainly was what prosecutors in Romania attempted in regards to the 2005 death of Sister Maricica.

15.2.2 Second-Degree Murder

The elements of second-degree murder and those for first-degree murder are identical. The requirement is that the government must prove that the accused killed a person, that the killing occurred with malice aforethought, and that the killing was premeditated. The difference is in the types of sentencing attached to each. Depending on the particular statute being applied, a sentence can include life but not death. The possibility of parole does exist in certain states and jurisdictions for second-degree murder.

Whether a person is charged with first- or second-degree murder really depends on the prosecutor. In most cases, the decision to prosecute second-degree murder hinges on what the prosecutor believes to be most achievable. He or she may prosecute a person for second-degree murder if it is believed that a conviction for first-degree would be difficult or would risk acquittal altogether. Second-degree murder has also been offered as a conviction option for a jury. Initial offers from the prosecution in regards to plea agreements will often start with a reduction to second-degree murder and a specific sentence term.

Second-degree murder charges resulting from a lethally botched exorcism is a possibility. But, the possibility of it being a conviction remains as slim as that for first-degree murder. The government's burden of proving malice aforethought and premeditation appears to be immensely difficult in a case of a person being killed during an exorcism or deliverance ritual. It is important to know and realize that there is always room for a change in that possibility.

15.3 CHILD ABUSE

There exists, throughout the governments of the world, many laws that define criminal conduct that involves the harming or killing of minors.

A minor is most commonly defined as any person under the age of eighteen years. In the United States, there is at least one case that includes the convicting of a Protestant minister for child abuse during an exorcism that resulted in serious harm and led to an eight-year-old boy's death. In cases of exorcism-related death of a person under the age of eighteen, the dual charges of manslaughter and child abuse or neglect is applicable.

In regard to these criminal laws, one is in high risk of being convicted if a subject or other person, under the age of eighteen, dies during an exorcism or deliverance effort. These laws are defined differently than manslaughter and murder are, and it is far easier for the government to prove their elements during a trial. Incidents that involve minors, especially small children, have a profound impact on jurors listening to and deciding on cases of alleged child abuse.

Child abuse charges can be prosecuted in addition to manslaughter or murder charges. It is also a charge that does not necessarily require the death of the victim, either. This means that if there is harm that is superficial or significant, but no death, then the exorcist and other participants may still be prosecuted for a dangerous or inappropriately executed ritual of exorcism or deliverance.

15.4 FALSE IMPRISONMENT AND KIDNAPPING

False imprisonment and kidnapping are very common criminal charges applied to cases involving inappropriate application of exorcism or deliverance services that result in harm or death. It is of grave importance that ministers, demonologists, and all others understand that if they hold a person against his or her will or move that person to a location against his or her will, then the crimes of kidnapping or false imprisonment can certainly be prosecuted against the perpetrating party. One should not rely on signed documents or releases for protection against prosecution for false imprisonment or kidnapping.

15.4.1 False Imprisonment

False imprisonment, most frequently listed as a misdemeanor crime, is commonly defined as unlawfully detaining or imprisoning of a person, against his or her will for any period of time.[3] Locking a person into a room or building, strapping a person to a chair or bed, or restricting a person's freedom of movement is the essence of false imprisonment. This detention occurs without legal authorization or justification.

Of course, there are, in certain jurisdictions, circumstances that could serve as an effective defense. For instance, a person who was severely intoxicated might be detained in order to prevent him or her from causing harm to self or others. A suicidal person might be held against his or her will long enough to get the person to a hospital and prevent the person from harming him- or herself. But, the deliberate detention of a person because of a belief that he or she has been possessed by demonic entities is difficult to assert as a defense in a courtroom dominated by secular concepts and procedures.

15.4.2 Kidnapping

A person is guilty of the crime of kidnapping when he or she unlawfully removes another person from their home or business in order to place that person substantially distant from where the person was found or unlawfully confines a person for any purpose or any period of time in a place of isolation.[4] If a minister or other accomplice to an exorcism team should, without legal justification or authorization, seize a person and take that person to any location in order to perform an exorcism and such was against the will of the seized person, then the crime of kidnapping has been committed.

Kidnapping is a very serious crime, so the absolute willingness of the subject, and all other participants, is essential to ensuring the legality and morality of any exorcism or deliverance effort. Beware of liability release statements and other similar documents, as many jurisdictions do not allow for a person to give irrevocable rights to any other person regarding confinement, restraint, or transport against the will of the person, where that person has decided to revoke or exercise a right to demand release or discontinuance of all activities. In other words, signed releases seldom protect the minister, church, group, supporters,

3. Dubber, *Criminal Law*, 383.
4. Dubber, *Criminal Law*, 382.

or others from liability or prosecution. Such documents are nothing more than vehicles of false security.

15.5 EXAMPLES OF PROSECUTION FOLLOWING BOTCHED EXORCISM

15.5.1 The Sister Maricica Exorcism Case

Twenty-three-year-old Sister Maricica Irina Cornici, an Orthodox Catholic nun, was severely troubled by disembodied voices. She believed that the voices were from Satan and reported to her friends that he accused her of great sin. The experiences were terrifying her and getting worse by the day. She arrived at the Holy Trinity convent in Tanacu, Romania, in late March 2005 to receive help in dealing with the experiences that were depriving her of much needed sleep and peace of mind. She confided in the nuns and priest, Father Daniel Petru Corogeanu, about the voices she was hearing.

By mid-April Sister Maricica was admitted to the Vaslui psychiatric hospital for evaluation and treatment after her behavior worsened to the point of violence and screaming. The voices were getting worse, and she was obsessed with the idea that the devil was telling her that she was a sinner. Dr. Gheoghe Silverstrovici was the attending psychiatrist who diagnosed the young nun with schizophrenic psychosis. After being medicated and stabilized, the nun was discharged from the hospital on April 20, 2005, and returned to the convent. An appointment was made for follow-up treatment in ten days. Sadly, she never made it to the appointment.

At some point after she returned to the convent, Sister Maricica began to relapse into a psychotic state and began to experience both visual and auditory hallucinations. She began to scream, speak incoherently, and began to act violently towards the other nuns. Father Daniel, the convent's priest, and four other nuns (Sisters Nicoleta Arcalianu, Adina Cepraga, Elena Otel, and Simona Bardana), became convinced that the young nun was possessed by Satan and decided to perform an exorcism ritual.[5] There was no formal investigation or determination process for demonic possession and no bishopric-level review or authorization

---

5. "Crucified Nun Dies in Exorcism," *BBC News*, June 18, 2005, http://news.bbc .co.uk/2/hi/europe/4107524.stm.

sought in the matter. Additionally, they did not call the psychiatrist or make arrangements to have Sister Maricica transported to the hospital for treatment.

During the course of the exorcism ritual, Sister Maricica was denied food and water. She was also chained to a cross in a crucifixion style within a dark, cold, and damp room. To dampen her screaming the nuns inserted a towel into her mouth to gag her. Because she would not drink holy water, Father Daniel refused her sustenance and medical treatment while keeping her chained to the cross. She was left alone in that condition for three days and died at some point within the three-day time period. The autopsy report indicated the cause of death to be asphyxiation.

This is not only a perfect example of misdiagnosed demonic possession but is also an example of negligent and brutal conduct on the part of the exorcist, Father Daniel Petru Corogeanu, and the four assisting nuns. There is absolutely no other way to view this incident as anything less than brutal, barbaric, and sadistic conduct. It is incidents like this that bring the importance of a mentally stable exorcist and exorcism team to the forefront.

Father Daniel, Sisters Nicoleta, Adina, Elena, and Simona were all charged with aggravated murder (equivalent to first-degree murder in the United States) by police officials in late June 2005. The charges were reduced to manslaughter, and each defendant was found guilty by a Bucharest court in February of 2007. Father Daniel received a fourteen-year imprisonment sentence, Sister Nicoleta received an eight-year jail sentence, and Sisters Adina, Elena, and Simona received five-year imprisonments.

The Romanian Orthodox Church, along with most of Romania, was shocked and appalled at the incident. The church issued an official statement that condemned the actions of Father Daniel Petru Corogeanu and promised reforms including stricter requirements on mental health evaluations for its priests. Additionally, the church banned Father Daniel from the priesthood and excommunicated him and the four nuns. Many in the village of Tanacu were in the courtroom praying for the four nuns and priest charged with manslaughter and even cried when the sentences were read out.

This incident is of remarkable similarity to the Anneliese Michel case of 1976. Anneliese Michel was diagnosed with psychosis of either the schizophrenic or bipolar form, and epilepsy, while Sister Maricica was diagnosed with schizophrenic psychosis. Both of these patients suffered from visual and auditory hallucinations and delusional thinking that included beliefs that Satan was speaking with them and that they were being made to suffer for sins. Even their ages are the same. And, their priests were all too ready to accept that the voices were demonic and not the product of mental illness without appropriate investigation and consideration for safety. How many other deaths have resulted from bizarre exorcisms based on misdiagnosed demonic possession in the thirty years that separate the deaths of Anneliese Michel and Sister Maricica?

15.5.2: Cottrell Exorcism Case

Eight-year-old Terrance Cottrell Jr., who suffered from autism and his mother went to Ray Hemphil, a Pentecostal minister, in August of 2004, hoping that the reverend would be able to help through religious services. Reverend Hemphil became convinced that the young boy was possessed by a demon or even Satan. He convinced the boy's mother that a deliverance service was required to rid the boy of the demon suspected of causing the autism.

During the exorcism ritual conducted by Reverend Hemphil, he laid across the boy's chest while singing or exclaiming prayers and demands for the demon to leave. Young Terrance was unable to breathe under the heavy weight of the hysterical preacher, and he died.[6] The autopsy report indicated that the boy died from asphyxiation.

Shortly after the boy's death, police charged the minister with physical abuse of a child resulting in severe harm. The Milwaukee, Wisconsin, judge sentenced Reverend Hemphil to thirty months imprisonment and ordered him not to conduct any exorcisms in the future. The boy's mother was distraught over the entire affair and was quoted by the press as saying that Terrance would still be with her if she had never taken him to that church.

This case certainly does not stand alone. It is only one of hundreds of deaths resulting from exorcism or deliverance efforts that are lacking in consideration for safety, well-being, health, sanity, and sound

---

6. "Man Sentenced to 30 Months After Botched Exorcism Ends in Death of Autistic Boy," *Christian Index*, September 9, 2004, http://christianindex.org/639.article.

common sense. There was no investigation, no involvement of medical science, no process of elimination followed, and no structured or safe method of exorcism executed. The ritual was invented, haphazard, and wreaked of negligence as the reverend went along. He killed an eight-year-old boy who was brought to him in faith and absolute trust by his mother. What victory for Christ was won in this abomination?

15.5.3 Zepeda Case

Gloria Galloway, a reporter for the *Globe and Mail* online, wrote an article about nineteen-year-old Walter Zepeda who died in Toronto following a protracted exorcism.[7] Walter had been at risk of falling into the life of gangs and drugs, and his behavior had begun to change drastically. He had begun to smoke cigarettes, listen to gang rap, and read magazines that contained satanic articles. His sister suffered from numerous mental health disorders and his older brother was in jail for drug trafficking. His father was desperate to deliver young Walter from these evil influences.

Walter's parents went to a local unidentified Protestant church for assistance in the matter. He told the minister that he was convinced that his son was possessed by the devil, and the minister gave instructions on how to carry out an exorcism. It isn't very clear if the minister took an active part in the ritual, but the parents certainly did. Walter was tied to a metal chair in the basement of their home while exorcism rites were performed nightly. He was denied all food and water throughout the seven day ordeal. When he began to scream too loudly, his mother and father duct taped his mouth shut. Walter Zepeda, aged only nineteen, died from dehydration.

The autopsy report indicated an emaciated state, loss of up to nine liters of body fluid, and listed the cause of death to be dehydration. Consequently, the authorities arrested the Zepeda parents and charged them with manslaughter. The father, Mr. Zepeda-Cordero, was sentenced to a compromised term of imprisonment, between the defense's suggested three years and the prosecution's requested five years. Walter's mother, Ana Mejia-Lopez, received a sentence of five hundred days, which was time already served in jail while awaiting trial.

---

7. Gloria Galloway, "Parents Sentenced for Exorcism Gone Wrong," *Globe and Mail*, May 23, 2003, http://www.rickross.com/reference/exorcism/exorcism8.html.

Again we see an example of negligence, hysteria, sadism, and ignorance in the application of exorcisms in America and throughout the rest of the world. Just as is seen in the Klingenberg case, Walter Zepeda died needlessly and torturously while his parents suffered both the loss of their son and criminal prosecution. The devil wins when the body of the afflicted is injured or killed. There is certainly no victory for humanity in the name of and in compliance with the will of God here.

PART 6

Means and Methods

A man's accomplishments in life are the cumulative effect of his attention to detail.

—John F. Dulles (1888–1959)

16

Administrative Affairs

16.1 CASE FILE ORGANIZATION

IN ORDER TO FUNCTION in a well-organized manner, regardless of purpose, cause, or security level involved, it is essential to have a standardized system for maintaining all evidence and records generated throughout the investigatory process, approval process, and exorcism process. The organization of case files can be achieved through a number of methods. Many demonologists and exorcists will utilize a method similar to that used by police detectives, while others have applied systems that resemble those used by hospitals and clinics. The organizational method used should place emphasis on both record security and ease of information reference and retrieval.

Case numbers allow for documents and other records to be associated with a particular case and prevent confusion between the document contents of different case files. As with the organizational methodology for case files, there are a number of ways to assign and track case numbers. The most basic form of case numbering is known as serial numbering and consists of simply assigning numbers to cases as they lay on a simple number line. An example would be 001, 002, 003, . . . , or 5451, 5452, 5453, ... Another method is to restrict serial numbering to within a twelve month period and distinguish repeating numbers by the year in which they were assigned. Such numbering would appear as 2010-001, 2010-002, 2010-003, ... Other case numbering systems involve more complex coding that refer to the type of case or incident region in conjunction with some sort of rolling or restricted serial numbering.

16.1.1 *The Investigative Process File*

It is recommended that the investigative file folder for any particular case be a classification folder that has at least two interior partitions and six total fasteners. This allows for the main six topics of information to be stored, using clasps, within a single file folder. Expanding classification folders for great document volumes are also available. A typical investigation that adheres to the requirement of thoroughness and completeness in information gathering will more commonly require the expanding versions of the classification file folder. Whether the folder is letter or legal sized is a matter of personal preference on the part of the investigator or exorcist and his or her organizational policies.

The investigative case folder should be broken down into six distinct categories. These categories are: (1) subject, witness, and other related persons; (2) incident history; (3) childhood and adult developmental history data; (4) subject medical history documents; (5) subject mental health history documentation; and (6) notes, statements, observations, and other related documentation. It is important that the investigative case folder contain only raw factual data and evidence. There should be no statements of interpretation of personal perspective of any sort placed in this folder.

16.1.2 *Review and Approval Process File*

The review and approval process records should be maintained in a separate folder under the same case number but labeled in such a way as to clearly identify it as the review process folder. It should also be a classification folder with six fasteners and two partitions. The first inside leaf should have the investigator's report with the investigator's conclusion. The second leaf should house the clerical peer review report and conclusion. The third leaf should hold the bishopric-level review and conclusion report, while the fourth leaf holds a copy of the bishop's authorization or denial for an exorcism or deliverance service. The fifth leave is where the bishop's order of assignment for a priest or minister to serve as the lead exorcist over the exorcism team is placed. This assignment must be accompanied by medical reports of sound mental and physical health from trained and licensed general health and separate mental health professionals. The roster of personnel who will serve in the various elements of the exorcism team is usually placed in the sixth leaf.

16.1.3 Exorcism or Deliverance Process File

All events, interviews, observations, and actions related to any approved exorcism or deliverance process should be recorded and filed in a separate file folder known as the exorcism process folder. This folder is labeled in such a manner as to distinguish it from the investigative and review process folders. The case number should also be placed on the file in order to ensure it is administratively associated with the correct case. It is recommended that this folder, like the investigative and review process folders, consist of a multileaf expandable classification folder.

The bishopric appointment letter, absent the medical records of the assigned exorcist, along with the approved exorcism team roster, should be affixed to the first leaf of the folder. Behind these documents should be all statements and memorandums of agreement, liability release forms, memorandum of being informed of and willing to perform the duties assigned to each exorcism team member, and consent to participate in an exorcism or deliverance ritual. These documents should be signed and notarized for the subject of the exorcism or deliverance and every member of the exorcism team.

The second page should include the investigator's report, the peer review report, and the bishopric-level review report. A copy of the physical and mental health evaluation reports are attached to the third leaf. In addition to the psychological and medical reports, a list of all conditions and medications currently being taken with doses and times should be included, as this will assist in relaying vital information to healthcare providers in the case of an emergency. It is important that the subject of the exorcism sign, and have notarized, a special power of attorney that assigns a specific person who will be readily available in a medical emergency as attorney-in-fact for the sole purpose of authorizing medical care and treatments for the subject if he or she is incapacitated.

The fourth leaf should hold copies of all letters and e-mails sent and received in relation to the exorcism or deliverance process. This includes letters and electronic correspondence by and between any member of the exorcism team and the bishopric-level supervising authority and any and all communications to other persons or organizations. The fifth leaf serves as a place for additional correspondence and activity records.

The most important record kept throughout the entire exorcism process is the *activity record*. This record documents every action and event on a minute-by-minute basis as they occur during every exorcism or deliverance session. The record is maintained in the exorcism process folder for the case on the sixth leaf, with the most recent entries shown at the top and the oldest entries on the bottom.

16.1.4 Audiovisual Recordings and Transcripts

References to tapes, memory items, and transcripts should be made in the activity record. Document numbers should be assigned to all correspondence, e-mail communications, audiovisual tapes and media, and all generated documents such as transcripts and diagrams in order to ensure appropriate reference. Audiovisual recordings should be stored separately in a manner that maintains functionality, security, and access by authorized personnel. The transcripts from recordings should be maintained in separate manila folders that are equipped with two-hole fasteners and not in the exorcism process folder.

16.2 REPORTS AND FORMS

16.2.1 Activity Record

There are many formats to use in recording the events that take place during exorcism and deliverance sessions. It is absolutely critical that accurate and complete records be maintained throughout the entire exorcism process, for spiritual, academic, and legal reasons. At the very least, the document should be headed with reference to the case and the subject, each entry must be numbered for future reference, and each entry should note the date and time for the event.

The event recorder (a member of the exorcism or deliverance team) is responsible for generating and maintaining the activity record and must be present at all exorcism sessions. Reliance on audiovisual recordings alone is insufficient, as typed personal observations serve as a data-preserving redundant practice. If audio tapes and transcripts are lost or damaged, then the activity report can be referenced as a credible record attested to by the event recorder.

Item#	Action/Entry	Date/Time
1	Meeting with the team, discussed psych records and testing w/team psychologist	01/05/11/1400
2	Field team met with Subjects parents and close family. Interview conducted and statements collected for review.	01/06/11/0931
3	Received digital video from field team observer. Subject displayed observable abnormal behavior. Footage sent via e-mail to team psychologist and lead priest for psychological and theological assessment.	01/07/11/0130

Figure 4. Activity record

16.2.2 Interview Reports

Interview reports are written in order to document encounters, conversations, and meetings by and between members of the investigative or exorcism teams and other people related to the case in question. This includes conversations with the subject, the subject's family members, the subject's normal church services minister, witnesses, specialists, and subject matter experts.

This document is written in professional letter or memorandum style and should always be typed. The interview report should include the date, time, and location of the interview. It should also identify who the interviewer is and who the main subject of the interview is. Additionally, all people present during the meeting should also be entered into the report. This report must cover the who, what, when, where, why, and how questions of any investigation or fact-finding effort.

The interview report covers conversations and meetings that exist or take place outside of the activity record coverage area. Vague or incomplete interview reports are useless and can sometimes be used against the exorcist in other proceedings or professional forums. It is greatly encouraged that these interviews and meetings be recorded as well as noted by the interviewing person. Be sure that all laws regarding the use of recording devices are followed in order to ensure that they may be used in all lawful activities following the interview. For instance, U.S. federal statutes require that only one party to a conversation be aware of the recording in order for it to be lawfully made and used ("one party rule"). However, each of the fifty states require either "the one party rule" (Georgia) or a "two/multiple party rule" (Florida), which means that all parties to the recorded conversation must be aware of and give consent to the recording before it is lawful. One should always be mindful of civil and criminal liability issues and work towards mitigating exposure as much as is legally and morally possible.

16.2.3 *Witness and Subject Statements*

Witnesses and the subject should always be encouraged, but not forced or coerced, to make formal written statements that attest to what they are reporting to the investigative authority. This provides a permanent record of what is being reported by the subject and all other witnesses. Statements should accompany interview reports and not be used in lieu of interview reports. Written witness statements allow for the creation of evidence that is used to support the evaluator's determinations, impressions, and assumptions regarding whether the individual is suffering from demonic possession and molestation or some physiological or mental ailment.

The person making the statement must be, to the best of the statement-collecting person's knowledge and belief, of sound mind and absent of any mind-altering drugs or medication. He or she should be encouraged to be as thorough and complete as possible while remaining absolutely factual throughout. If the person can't remember a detail with too much clarity or certainty, then he or she should state that and not guess or make up anything. It is highly recommended that these statements be witness-signed and notarized official documents.

Should the reasoning of the evaluator, priest, exorcist, or demonologist ever come into academic, professional, or legal question, then these statements may serve as supporting evidence in demonstrating how and upon what grounds certain decisions, determinations, and actions were taken by the clerical exorcist, members of the exorcism team, or others involved or related to the case. The general rule of thumb is that if it isn't documented, then it didn't happen.

17

Holy Items

I N VIRTUALLY ALL CATHOLIC and Catholic-like faiths, the use of special holy items during the execution of an exorcism or similar ritual is absolutely necessary. Such items as a crucifix, holy water sprinkling, class-two relics, communion ware, and others are used in the confrontation with the forces of evil. A holy item can be a physical item, such as a crucifix or saint's medallion, or a spoken or sung chant or gospel reading. These items are indeed holy and must be treated with the highest regard and reverence at all times. They should also be maintained in a manner that prevents them from being damaged or defiled by the afflicted person during an exorcism session.

Holy items perform and represent certain aspects of Christian identity and the power of the Holy Spirit. Thus, they become powerful weapons against the unclean spirits that seek to occupy and tormentingly command the bodies of the faithful and not-so-faithful alike.

17.1 HOLY WATER

Holy Water has been a substance of great religious importance since the days of Jesus's baptism in the Jordan River. It is used in many rituals throughout Christendom's many denominations. The means of blessing and the origins of sanctified waters vary from faith to faith, but holy water remains a central figure in all of them. Indeed, it is the most powerful spiritual and symbolic item for Christians.

There are two ways for water to become holy in the Christian faith. The first is known as *water of holy origin* and the second is known as *water of holy blessing*. Water that comes from the Jordan River, sanctified places, or miraculous springs are considered holy in origin and thus already blessed directly by the hand of God, the creator of all that is. Water originating from other nonsanctified springs or holy places is blessed through a sacred ritual, usually by a priest or bishop and is then transcended into holiness through the presence of the Holy Spirit and the will of the Lord God.

17.1.1 *Water of Holy Origin*

Water of holy origin can be collected from places known to be both holy and able to miraculously heal people. Water from the Jordan River in Israel is water that flows over holy ground because it was in this river that Jesus Christ, the Holy Son of God, the creator of all that was, is, and will be, was baptized and declared to be in the Lord's favor. It is believed by many to be the absolute most potent of the holy waters. Other springs such as that at Lourdes in France, Mother Cabrini Spring in Colorado, and Fatima Fountain in Portugal also provide sanctified waters for use in ritual and healing. In older times, one would have to travel to the springs to collect their waters, but today it can be done with the click of a mouse over the internet.

17.1.2 *Water of Holy Blessing*

Water of holy blessing can be created through the execution of a special prayer and ritual that is normally conducted by a minister, priest, or bishop. Through this process, the water is transformed from ordinary to spiritually extraordinary through the power of the Holy Spirit and the will of the Lord, our God. The following is a procedure for the creation of holy water through the pre-1984 Catholic rite and serves as wonderful example of the transition prayer effect:

> 1. On Sundays, or whenever this blessing takes place, salt and fresh water are prepared in the church or in the sacristy. The priest, vested in surplice and purple stole, says:
>
> P: Our help is in the name of the Lord.

All: Who made heaven and earth.

2. The exorcism of salt follows:

God's creature, salt, I cast out the demon from you by the living †God, by the true †God, by the holy †God, by God who ordered you to be thrown into the water-spring by Eliseus to heal it of its barrenness. May you be a purified salt, a means of health for those who believe, a medicine for body and soul for all who make use of you. May all evil fancies of the foul fiend, his malice and cunning, be driven afar from the place where you are sprinkled. And let every unclean spirit be repulsed by Him who is coming to judge both the living and the dead and the world by fire.

All: Amen.

Let us pray.

Almighty everlasting God, we humbly appeal to your mercy and goodness to graciously bless †this creature, salt, which you have given for mankind's use. May all who use it find in it a remedy for body and mind. And may everything that it touches or sprinkles be freed from uncleanness and any influence of the evil spirit; through Christ our Lord.

All: Amen.

Exorcism of the water:

God's creature, water, I cast out the demon from you in the name of God †the Father almighty, in the name of Jesus † Christ, His Son, our Lord, and in the power of the Holy † Spirit. May you be a purified water, empowered to drive afar all power of the enemy, in fact, to root out and banish the enemy himself, along with his fallen angels. We ask this through the power of our Lord Jesus Christ, who is coming to judge both the living and the dead and the world by fire.

All: Amen.

Let us pray.

O God, who for man's welfare established the most wonderful mysteries in the substance of water, hearken to our prayer, and pour forth your blessing on this †element now being prepared with various purifying rites. May this creature of yours, used in your mysteries and endowed with your grace, serve to cast out demons and to banish disease. May everything that this water sprinkles in the homes and gatherings of the faithful be delivered from all that is unclean and hurtful; let no breath of contagion hover there, no taint of corruption; let all the wiles of the lurking enemy come to nothing. By the sprinkling of this water may everything opposed to the safety and peace of the occupants of these homes be banished, so that in calling on your holy name they may know the well-being they desire, and be protected from every peril; through Christ our Lord.

All: Amen.

3. Now the priest pours the salt into the water in the form of a cross, saying:

May this salt and water be mixed together; in the name of the Father†, and of the Son†, and of the Holy † Spirit.

All: Amen.

P: The Lord be with you.
All: And with thy spirit.

Let us pray.

God, source of irresistible might and king of an invincible realm, the ever-glorious conqueror; who restrains the force of the adversary, silencing the uproar of his rage, and valiantly subduing his wickedness; in awe and humility we beg you, Lord, to regard with favor this creature thing of salt and water, to let the light of your kindness shine upon it, and to hallow it with the dew of your mercy; so that wherever it is sprinkled and your holy name is invoked, every assault of the unclean spirit may be baffled, and all dread of the serpent's venom be cast out. To us who entreat your mercy grant that the Holy Spirit may be with us wherever we may be, through Christ our Lord.

All: Amen.[1]

17.2 ANOINTING OILS

Anointing oils have been used since long before the days of our Savior and Lord, Jesus Christ. From the earliest dating Judaic records it is learned that special and sanctified oils have been used in worship, blessing, healing, assignment, and empowering rituals. Even the dead were anointed with holy oils just before their internment. Holy oils, like holy

---

1. "Blessing of Water in Traditional and New Rite," in the *Roman Ritual*. Holy Family Catholic Church, www.daytonlatinmass.org/wp-content/uploads/2009/05/blessing-of-water.pdf.

water, are very ancient and powerful tools. Some Christian and Judaic sects have very specific formulas, or recipes, for the creation of special religious oils.

17.2.1 *Types and Categories of Anointing Oils*

Many different oils are used throughout the practices of Christianity. For many faiths, each oil type has a different purpose and strength, while others use only a specific type to cover all issues of the spirit and faith. Anointings are used more in Protestant Christian faiths in deliverance efforts. The most common types of anointing oils are, frankincense and myrrh oil, frankincense oil, King Solomon oil, Rose of Sharon oil, spikenard anointing oil, cinnamon anointing oil, and olive oil.

While there are many types of anointing oils, there are also two categories of holy oils. These are *oils of holy origin* and *oils of holy blessing*. As with holy water, the difference is found in the origin of the oil. For instance, olive, frankincense, and myrrh oils that were extracted from plants that grew in the Holy Land (Israel) originate from the sacred soil of a holy place and were watered by the same holy waters that baptized the Son of God, Jesus Christ. Therefore, these oils are holy and sacred in their own right and in some faiths require no additional blessing prayer or ritual. On the other hand are oils that were not extracted from plants that grew in the Holy Land but are indeed the oils proscribed for sacred ritual. These oils attain their spiritual consecration and power via special blessing rites and prayers performed by Jewish rabbis and Christian priests, ministers, and bishops.

17.2.2 *Where to Find Religious Anointing Oils*

Acquiring anointing oils today isn't as difficult or time consuming as it once was. There are a number of internet sites where these oils can be purchased in varying volumes directly from the makers in Israel. These internet sites can be found by searching for anointing oils through a reputable search engine. Be sure to shop around, as there are many reputable Israeli and Italian suppliers who compete fiercely in regards to per volume pricing.

17.2.3 Blessing Anointing Oils

Just as there are many different types of oils, there are also many ways in which they are blessed for ritual and other religious applications. Some methods involve elaborate rituals with long and complicated prayers of blessing while other approaches involve a simple prayer for blessing. In the Roman anointing rite a simple prayer is said while the priest extends his right hand over the oil being blessed.[2] Below is a common blessing for anointing oils and is useful across all Catholic and Protestant denominations:

1. The priest/minister/bishop places the vessel of oil on a royal purple cloth in front of a standing crucifix or Christ icon.

2. The priest/minister/bishop then places his right hand over the vessel containing the oil and recites the following prayer:

Priest: Glory be to the †Father, to the †Son, and to the Holy † Spirit.

All: Amen

Priest: Lord, God Almighty, maker of all that was, is, and will be, we stand before you in awe and praise of your never ending glory. May it be pleasing to you, this oil, that you may bless it and fill it with the power of the Holy † Spirit. Lord God, may you be pleased with this oil and through your glorious power and will ordain it for the healing of the sick, strengthening of the weak, protection of the vulnerable, and deliverance of the afflicted from the clutches of evil. We ask this in the name of your Holy Son, Jesus † Christ, who stands at your right hand in heaven forever.

All: Amen.

Priest: This oil is consecrated in the name of the †Father, and of the †Son, and of the Holy † Spirit.

All: Amen.

17.3 CRUCIFIX

17.3.1 The Holy Crucifix

A crucifixion was an ancient form of torturous public execution. It was utilized extensively by ancient Rome and other similarly dated civilizations as a means of making a horrid and terrifying example out of those

2. *Pastoral Care of the Sick*, 110.

who challenged the regime or refused to follow its laws. The idea was to use fear as a means of forcing conformity upon subjects or oppressed people by a particular ruling class or government. Today, this tactic would be known as a form of terrorism or even a crime against humanity. It certainly qualifies as being a cruel and excessive form of punishment even for those deserving death as a punishment for their crime.

A crucifixion involved the nailing of the condemned person to a wooden cross or X- or T-shaped device that kept the hands and arms outstretched and the legs affixed to the standing staff or legs of the cross as the case may be. It was an extremely slow and painful death for anyone put through this. Death usually occurred through suffocation as the person lost the ability to hold himself up enough to breathe. It was this device and means of execution that was used to kill our Lord and Savior, the holy Son of God, Jesus Christ.

The crucifix is a representation of Christ's agony on the cross. Its most common appearance is of two beams, one shorter than the other, placed perpendicular to one another. The longer beam is vertical and centered on the shorter beam that is horizontal. The horizontal beam is off center to the vertical beam. The arrangement is similar to a lower case "t" shape. Affixed to this cross is the image of Christ nailed to the cross. Other representations include the tau cross that is shaped like a capital "T" with the image of Christ affixed as he would have appeared during his crucifixion. These crucifixes are made in all sizes and in all materials. The most common is carved wood. Many pendant-sized crucifixes are made of precious metals and can be seen adorned with precious and semiprecious stones.

The Roman rite of exorcism does call for the use and presence of a crucifix during all sessions. Protestant ministers are also known to frequently use crucifixes and crosses as a part of their deliverance or exorcism ritual. For the purposes of driving out or driving away demonic entities, the crucifix, in comparison to the simple cross, is the most powerful tool as it is a direct representation of the Lord, Jesus Christ in his most passionate condition.

17.3.2 The Holy Cross

The holy cross is a simple representation of the mechanism of crucifixion and does not depict the crucifixion itself. It normally consists of two beams, one shorter than the other, which are crossed perpendicularly. The longer vertical beam is centered on the shorter horizontal beam but the horizontal beam is positioned off-center and towards the top of the vertical beam.

Simple crosses are made of many different types of materials. The most common materials are wood and precious metals. They are also made in any size, from necklace pendants to large steeple tops. The simple cross remains a very sacred item as it represents the instrument through which the Lord Jesus Christ shed his blood for the forgiveness of all of humanity's transgressions. For many people, the simple or naked cross is symbolic of their having taken up the cross to follow Christ's mission and teachings.

17.4 RELICS

Sacred relics have been used by the earliest known Christian churches as parts of various rituals and traditions throughout history. Indeed, even today one can find relics in churches, special museums, and private collections. A booming business in ancient artifacts has been maintained for over one thousand years, with its peak happening during the Crusades.

There are three classifications of holy relics recognized by the Vatican, patriarchs of the many orthodox churches, and offshoot Catholic-like churches alike. Class-one relics are those items that come from the body of a saint or holy martyr. Class-two relics are those items that were worn, touched, or in some way used by the saints or martyrs of the holy Christian Church, and class-three relics are those items that have been touched by a class-two or class-three relic and absorb that higher classed relic's grace or spiritual power.

Class-one relics are the highest and obviously most powerful of the relic classes. These consist of actual body parts of the saints or special martyrs. A piece of the true cross is also a class-one relic. When a saint died in the Middle Ages, he or she was quickly mutilated following beatification in order to provide class-one relics to the many churches of faithful people. Such a relic could be a splinter of bone from a saint, a finger, hand, or even head of a saint. It wasn't seen then, as it is today, as a very disrespectful and morbid practice. The Roman Church has absolutely forbade the sale or trade of class-one relics, but the practice continues at this very moment throughout Russia and the Middle East.

Class-two relics are those items that were worn, used routinely, or touched in some special way by a saint or martyr. A rosary used by a saint on a routine basis, or a mere piece of that rosary, can easily become a class-two relic. The clothes or vestments worn by a saint or martyr, or pieces thereof, are also considered class-two relics. These relics, like the class-one relics, have been forbidden for trade or profiteering by the Vatican and several other churches, like the Anglican Church. But, as with the others, this trade flourishes throughout Russia and the Middle East. This is especially so for Palestine, Israel, Syria, and Egypt.

As relics go, the easiest relics to produce and acquire lie in the class-three area. These relics are any item that has been touched to any class-one or class-two relic. A ring or religious medallion touched to the mummified hand of Mary Magdalene, maintained at the Orthodox Church of Saint Mary Magdalene (in the Garden of Gethsemane on the Mount of Olives) is considered to have absorbed the piousness and holy nature of the saint and thus becomes a relic of its own sort. It is this form of relic that is categorized as a class-three relic. Class-three relics are openly and widely traded. Many can be purchased directly from the Roman (Vatican-controlled) churches that control all, or most, of the available class-one and class-two relics.

What appears at first glance to be an attempt to be responsible and more caring of holy relics or the attempt to discontinue profiting from such relics by the Roman Catholic Church is nothing more than a maneuver to corner the market. The church controls access to all of the relics and then touches, if they really do that at all, medals and medallions, crosses, and rosaries to them in order to fetch tremendous revenues from paying visitors to museums and gullible followers of the faith who encounter the trinket sellers around every corner in every religious pilgrimage place. For many, this practice wreaks of the money changers whose tables Jesus overturned in Jerusalem in the temple so many years ago.

In combating the elements of the demonic world, class-two and greater relics should be used, as there are a plethora of examples where class-three relics only made the demonic entity laugh. The demon was able to say what tomb, tunic, or saintly artifact was touched by the class three-relic, and relic was ridiculed as nothing more than a trinket. Where such relics are unavailable, there is no reason to despair, as water of holy origin, especially from the River Jordan, has tremendous impact on demoniacal elements in or near the human body.

17.5 ATTIRE

What is physically worn during a deliverance service or ritual by most Protestant ministers and lay ministers is unimportant in comparison to wearing the Holy Spirit's armor in the face of evil. So, one more commonly encounters ministers in a simple shirt and pair of blue jeans during a deliverance rather than in full vestments as is worn during Sunday services. This isn't always the case though, as many show up in suits and even in pulpit robes to confront evil and eliminate its grasp of the afflicted person.

For Catholic, Orthodox, and other nondiocese-related Catholic churches, the case is significantly different. Priests perform exorcisms as proscribed by the *Rituale Romanum* and other Orthodox rules while wearing full vestments under color purple. For these faithful followers of Christ, the clerical shirt and suit is insufficient for deliberate encounters with Satan and his millions of subordinate demons. The vestments are endowed with special spiritual power and afford the priest with additional authoritative and protective power against the demonic realm.

What is worn really depends on the minister and the particular type of Christian faith he or she practices. Many exorcists and deliverance ministers have reported experiencing more difficulty in driving away demonic entities when the services were performed without the use of worn vestments or holy apparel. It certainly doesn't hurt to be dressed for battle, so to speak, when confronting possessing entities.

18

Prayers and Rites

THIS CHAPTER COVERS THOSE prayers that are most commonly used by Orthodox, Roman, and Protestant faiths during exorcisms or deliverance rituals. The intent is to provide the deliverance minister with prayer options and examples that are known to have been quite effective against demoniacal elements bent on tormenting the innocents of God's creation. It is important to note that these prayers are useless unless the minister is open to the Holy Spirit and has been filled with its power and determination.

18.1 COMMONLY USED PRAYERS

18.1.1 The Lord's Prayer

The Lord's Prayer has been seen in many different forms and in many different languages. This is mainly due to both interpretations of ancient texts and the style of writing used to present the interpretations. This prayer is two thousand years old and was first spoken by the Lord Jesus Christ himself as he taught his apostles, disciples, and followers the proper way to pray. Every Christian from that day through to the present has been taught this prayer and has prayed it countless times for themselves and others. The following is but one version of this most special and powerful prayer:

Our Father in heaven, hallowed be your name, your kingdom
come, your will be done, on earth as it is in heaven. Give us today
our daily bread; and forgive us our debts, as we forgive our debt-
ors, and do not subject us to the final test, but deliver us from the
evil one. (Matt 6:9)

18.1.2 Fatima Prayer of Oh My Jesus

O my Jesus, I offer this for love of thee, for the conversion of
sinners and the reparation for the sins committed against the immaculate heart of Mary. Amen.

18.1.3 Hail Mary

The prayer that hails the Virgin Marry is extracted from the story of the
Immaculate Conception found in the New Testament Book of Luke 1:28.
When the Angel of the Lord, Gabriel, approached the Blessed Virgin
he exclaimed, "Hail, Mary! The Lord is with thee." This proclamation is
clearly seen as being incorporated into the intercessional prayer to the
Holy Virgin Mary, the Mother of Jesus. This prayer is very well known
by Roman and Roman-like Catholics around the world but not so much
by Protestants. The most common form of the prayer is:

Hail Mary, full of grace! The Lord is with thee. Blessed art thou
among women and blessed is the fruit of thy womb, Jesus. Holy
Mary, Mother of God, pray for us sinners now and at the hour of
our death. Amen.

18.1.4 Blessed Be Prayer

Blessed be the †Father and the Son and the Holy Spirit. As it was
in the beginning is now and ever shall be, world without end.
Amen.

18.1.5 *Prayer to a Guardian Angel for Oneself*

A person's guardian angel is the first line of defense against the elements of evil. Angelic influence and strength in dealing with diabolic attacks against the protected person is dependent upon the piousness and innocence of the individual. In situations where the individual has led a life of absolute sin and disregard for the laws of God, there may be no assistance available at all from a guardian. An angel will be present but unable to engage demonic entities who, through the sin of the individual, have a rightful claim to punitively torment him or her. This is not to say that humans who are less than perfect will have no protection from the devil but rather that those who grossly turn away from God and willfully and wantonly violate the divine decrees have made themselves rightful targets for demonic infestation or contamination.

No human is perfect, and God knows this more than anyone in the universe. Below is a prayer that is commonly used to call on the protective angels for intercession and guidance:

> Bless the Lord, all you his angels, you who are mighty in strength and do his will. Intercede for me at the throne of God, and by your unceasing watchfulness protect me in every danger of soul and body.[1] Obtain for me the grace of final perseverance, so that after this life I may be admitted to your glorious company and may sing with you the praises of God for all eternity.
>
> O all you holy angels and archangels, thrones and dominations, principalities and powers and virtues of heaven, cherubim and seraphim and especially you, my dear guardian angel, intercede for me and obtain for me the special favor I now ask. [State your intention here.]
>
> [Follow this with the Lord's Prayer.]

18.1.6 *Prayer to Guardian Angels for Friends*

All Christians are encouraged to pray frequently for others as well as themselves. As has been stated numerous times in this book already, prayer is the most powerful tool humanity has in achieving forgiveness, redemption, and help during crises. Praying for others to be guided and protected by their guardian angels will result in their being saved from

---

1. This first section can be repeated a second time.

tremendous harm or hardship. Below is an example of a prayer to another's guardian angel and is but one of hundreds of such prayers:

> Guardian Angel, watch over those whose names you can read in my heart. Guard over them with every care and make their way easy and their labors fruitful. Dry their tears if they weep; sanctify their joys; raise their courage if they weaken; restore their hope if they lose heart, their health if they be ill, truth if they err, and repentance if they fail. Amen.

18.1.7 Prayer to Saint Michael the Archangel

The archangel Michael is God's military field marshal. He, along with his tens of thousands of lesser angels, subdued the rebellious Lucifer, and his lesser demons, and cast him into the depths of hell. It is this angel whose power is immediately supreme over the demoniacal elements of the spiritual and physical realms. His power is bested only by the Lord Jesus Christ and the Holy Father, God Almighty. Invoking Saint Michael and asking for his intercession in dealing with demons is of particular importance for both deliverance and exorcism efforts. The most common prayer, recited for hundreds of years by Catholic Christians, is:

> Holy Michael, the Archangel, defend us in battle. Be our safeguard against the wickedness and snares of the devil. May God rebuke him, we humbly pray; and do you, O Prince of the heavenly host, by the power of God, cast into hell Satan and all the evil spirits who wander through the world seeking the ruin of souls. Amen.

18.1.8 The Sign of the Cross

In the name of the †Father, and of the Son, and of the Holy Spirit. Amen.

18.1.9 Deliverance or Petit Exorcism Prayer

Priest: In the name of Jesus Christ, our Lord and God, strengthened by the intercession of the Virgin Mary, Mother of Jesus, of the Archangel Michael, of the Apostles Peter and Paul, of all the Saints, and the authority of our holy ministry, we confidently undertake to reject and expel the attacks and deceit of the devil.

Priest: God arises; His enemies are scattered like ash in the wind and flee before Him. As wax melts before the fire, so too shall the wicked perish at the presence of God.

Priest: (Holding the Crucifix) Behold the Cross of the Lord, flee all you enemies of God!

All: The Lion of the Tribe of Judah, the offspring of David has conquered you.

Priest: May your mercy descend upon us, oh Lord.

All: As great as our hope in you, Lord, we drive out the Dark One from us, unclean spirits, all satanic powers, all wicked legions, assemblies, and sects.

Priest: In the name and by the power of our Lord Jesus Christ, †may you be snatched away and driven from the Church of God and from the souls made to the image and likeness of God and redeemed by the Precious Blood of the Divine Lamb. †Most cunning serpent, you shall no more dare to deceive the human race, persecute the Church, torment God's elect, and sift them as wheat. †The Most High God commands you! †He with whom, in your great insolence, you still claim to equal. (Priest reads 1 Tim 2:4.)

Priest: God the Father commands you! †God the Son commands you! †God the Holy Spirit commands you!

Priest: †Christ, God's Word made Flesh, commands you! †He who to save our race outdone through your envy, "humbled Himself, becoming obedient even unto death." †He who has built His Church on the firm rock and declared that the gates of hell shall not prevail against Her, because He will dwell with Her, "all days even to the end of the world."

Priest: The Sacred Sign of the Cross commands you, †as does also the power of the mysteries of the Christian Faith. †The glorious Mother of God, the Virgin Mary, commands you! †The blood of the martyrs and the pious intercession of the Saints command you! †The faith of the apostles Peter and Paul, along with all of the other Apostles, commands you!

Priest: Thus, cursed dragon, and you, diabolical legions, we adjure you by the living God, †by the true God, †by the Holy God, †by the God who so loved the world that he gave up His only Son, that every soul believing in him might not perish but have life everlasting. Stop deceiving human creatures and pouring out to them the poison of eternal damnation! Stop harming the Church and hindering Her liberty!

Priest: Be gone, Satan, creator and master of all deceit, adversary of man's salvation! Give place to Christ in whom you have found no works of your sort. Give place the One, Holy, Christian Church ordained by Jesus Christ through His Precious and Holy Blood. Stoop beneath the omnipotent hand of God Almighty. Tremble and flee as we exclaim the Holy name of Jesus whose name causes hell to tremble!

Priest: Oh Lord, most compassionate, hear our prayer.

All: And let my cry come to you.

Priest: May the Lord be with you.

All: And with your spirit.

Priest: Oh Lord, the creator of all that was, is, and will be, grant us your powerful protection, expel the unclean spirits that torment and tempt us, and keep us safe and sound. We ask this through you Holy Son, Jesus Christ, who reigns with you in heaven forever.

All: Amen.

18.2 COMMON BIBLICAL READINGS

Biblical Scripture, especially when it quotes the Lord Jesus Christ, is powerful against the demonic world. Reading the Scriptures brings to mind the power and majesty of the Son of God and through him is delivered the Holy Spirit and the strength of heaven's angelic legions. The readings included in this chapter are not only the most commonly heard exorcism and deliverance readings but are among the most powerful as inspiration and strength for humans and as a shield and weapon against the Dark One.

The reading of these holy writings must be in the highest level of reverence. Never should there be any act or omission that serves to reduce the majesty of the Lord our God, or that may, in actuality or appearance, present disrespect at any level. If there is among the members of the exorcism team any person who is less than absolutely reverent and respectful to the holy items and Scriptures, then that person should not be chosen to read during the ritual of exorcism or deliverance. In fact, such a person can serve more as a detriment to the team and the effort against evil possession than an asset.

The Roman rite of exorcism contains a long list of biblical readings that are designed to drive out demons. This driving out occurs either through the reminder of the greatness of their holy foe or through the invocation and enhancement of the holy presence through the readings. This is applicable to Protestant approaches against demons, also. Regardless of which effect prevails in the confrontation, there is absolutely no doubting that the reading of the Gospels has profound power over the demoniacal elements of the universe.

Table 2. Scripture readings in exorcism and deliverance

Psalm 3
Psalm 10
Psalm 12
Psalm 21
Psalm 30
Psalm 34
Psalm 53
Psalm 67
Psalm 69
Psalm 90
Psalm 117
Mark 16:15–18
Luke 10:17–20
Luke 11:14–22
John 1:1–14

19

Indicators of Possession

THERE ARE THOUSANDS OF cases throughout history that undoubtedly are not of the here but of the hereafter or the realm beyond our current senses and definable by current science. In reviewing many of these cases, which are most likely classifiable as demonic, there is a pattern of conduct that can be observed. These similarities in conduct from one case to another allow for an accurate compilation of symptoms that may be used in determining whether or not a person has been afflicted with demoniacal molestation, possession, or influence.

19.1 STRENGTH AND POWERS BEYOND THE NORMAL HUMAN CONDITION

The display of strength and power that goes beyond the normal human condition mentioned in the *Rituale Romanum* is not restrictive to physical strength. The definition of this condition includes demonstrated capabilities that go beyond known physics and human design. For instance, the person may be able to read minds (telepathy) or cause things to move without having to physically act upon them (telekinesis). Another example, reported in many cases, is of activities that violate physics, like crawling up the walls or walking on the ceiling.

19.1.1 *Superhuman Strength and Agility*

A person possessed by elements of the diabolical may display signs and symptoms that include incredible physical strength. A 90-pound young lady who could barely bench press 50 pounds can now suddenly lift and throw a 220-pound grown man across the room or lift 150-pound solid wood furniture. This condition is almost unanimously reported in highly credible cases of demonic possession. Malachi Martin has addressed the condition of superhuman physical strength in his book, *Hostage to the Devil* and in numerous news and talk show interviews.

Superhuman agility, or extraphysiological ability (EPA, pronounced in short as "ehpah"), is another characteristic discussed by a plethora of demonologists and exorcists around the world. This condition involves the body's ability to bend and contort into positions that, under normal conditions, would severely injure or even kill the possessed individual. These hideous physiological contortions are described as terrifying when seen in person. Indeed, the average person cannot possibly begin to seriously accept such a possibility without actually seeing it happen. This is especially so when the afflicted person is delivered from demonic control without any serious or permanent injuries that would surely have resulted from bending backwards to a point where both ends of the body (feet and head) touch the floor simultaneously. This is such an unfathomable condition that even photographs and video footage is immediately dismissed as fraudulent.

Another little-known term but well-heard of condition is ultraphysical ability (UPA, pronounced as "yoopah"). This is the ability to leap beyond the restrictions of established physical laws. Indeed, this may be the one most shocking and unnerving condition observed in a case of demoniacal possession. The UPA condition is described in many stories of severe possession and involves the person's ability to crawl or walk up walls and across ceilings. It can also include hovering or floating as if in a weightless environment.

Some rare cases of possession have reported the combined presence of EPA and UPA that caused many a person (including some clergymen), in the words of General George S. Patton, to "un-ass the area of operation in quick haste" upon witnessing the event. It is easily agreed that the sight of a person whose body is contorted beyond its design and resembles a crab or spider crawling up the wall is a most unusual, terrifying, and difficult to believe situation. Describing what has been witnessed to others who have not personally witnessed the event is near impossible and often results in the person being subjected to accusations of deceit or fabrication and of cruel ridicule. Nevertheless, there are those, including members of the clergy, who swear to this type of thing happening.

Certain conditions can also be indicative of the type and strength of entity being confronted. That is definitely the case regarding EPA or UPA presence. Many experts in the fields of theology and demonology have expressed a belief that the presence of either ability is ominous. These experts assert that these abilities are presented when the entity in possession of the victim is not of the lower demonic echelons but of the principalities. Such a confrontation is said to present enhanced physical and spiritual dangers for everyone involved in the exorcism effort.

19.1.2 Telekinesis

In its most basic definition, the word *telekinesis* refers to the ability to move objects without physically or mechanically acting on them. It is a subcategory of psychokinesis, which refers to the solely mental ability to affect physical objects. A telekinetic person can, according to prevailing theories in parapsychology, cause objects to levitate, move, or change their physical characteristics through thought alone.

In regards to demonic possession, the afflicted will, while under the control of the evil entity, cause pictures to fly off of the walls and objects on desks and draws to become projectiles through thought alone. This is evidenced usually, according to many experts, by the afflicted person's gazing or concentrating on the object just before it moves. Some cases have included reports of the individual, while the demon is in dormancy, being able to effectively exercise telekinetic activity. The telekinetic capability of a person, who otherwise doesn't have such ability, is substantially indicative of demonic infestation.

19.1.3 Telepathy

Telepathy is distinguished as an ability to receive or transmit thoughts through means that lay outside the traditional five senses of the human body. A telepath is said to be able to detect another person's thoughts, read another person's memories, or transmit thoughts or impressions to another. Telepathy is also a subcategory of psychokinesis, along with telekinesis (section 19.2.2).

In cases of demonic possession, the afflicted person or controlling demon may answer statements that were only thought by a person and not, in anyway, verbalized or communicated. An example of this would be a member of an exorcism team who starts thinking about his mother without saying anything when the demon, or afflicted person, suddenly asks aloud why the person is concerned with his mother. Another example can be seen when the demonic entity starts screaming to shut up when someone starts reciting a prayer or bible verse mentally.

19.1.4 Clairvoyance

Clairvoyance is described as being the ability to receive information regarding the past, present, and future through means other than those of physical presence, the five senses, or learned or known of through other resources or means. The word is made through the combining of the two French words of *clair*, meaning "clear," and *voyance*, meaning "vision" or "view." In essence, the word *clairvoyance* translates to "clear vision" or "clear view." There are four subcategories to clairvoyance, which are retrocognition, precognition, mediumship, and remote viewing.

19.1.4.1 Retrocognition

Retrocognition is defined as the ability to detect and relay the details of a past event through methods beyond the five senses and in complete absence of any personal knowledge of the subject. A retrocognitive person may be able to disclose details about an unsolved murder that would be known only by the investigating officers, the victims, and the killer one hundred or more years after the crime occurred. Such details are usually verifiable through historical and investigative research.

Edgar Cayce, the famous clairvoyant, is believed to have been able to go into the past and describe details about events not commonly known but verifiable by historical researchers. His most famous unverified retrocognitive statements are in reference to the fabled lost city of

Atlantis and the activities of Atlantean survivors.[1] It is believed that he successfully described the city, its location, and the means by which it was destroyed.

19.1.4.2 Precognition

Precognition is the exact opposite of retrocognition in that it involves a person's ability to see events and conditions that have not yet come to pass. Precognitive people are said to have an ability to accurately predict the future in regards to particular people, groups, places, events, or virtually anything. The *Rituale Romanum* recognizes the ability to tell future events with accuracy as a symptom or indicator of a demonic presence or influence. This perspective is shared with a number of demonological experts and Protestant Christian ministers.

One of the most famous precognitive people in all of history is Nostradamus, or Michel de Nostradame, who lived in France from 1503 to 1566. It is believed by many that Nostradamus was able to successfully see and record visions of the future in poetic quatrains that have, over time, come to be with exceptional likeness to his descriptions/predictions. He is credited with having predicted Napoleon, Adolf Hitler, and even the Kennedy assassination.[2] However, there is a long line of academics, theologians, ministers, and scientists who doubt his ability to accurately see future events.[3]

19.1.4.3 Mediumship, or Necromancy

A medium is a person who is believed to be able to communicate with the spirits of long-dead human beings, heavenly entities, and elements of the diabolical realm. *Mediumship*, or *necromancy*, is the practice or routine communication with the dead or other spiritual entities by a person or group of people said to be "sensitive to spiritual energies." Necromancy is often practiced through means and mechanisms such

1. "Edgar Cayce's Readings on Ancient Mysteries," Edgar Cayce's A.R.E., http://www.edgarcayce.org/arc/ancient_mysteries.aspx.

2 "Nostradamus," Nastrodamus.org, http://www.nostradamus.org/bio.php.

3. Kendrick Frazier, "Commentary: Clear Thinking and the Forces of Unreason," *Skeptical Inquirer* 26, no. 2, 2002, http://www.csicop.org/si/show/commentary_clear_thinking_and_the_forces_of_unreason/.

as Wiccan rituals, satanic rituals, voodoo rituals, Ouija boards, crystal balls, pendulums, and meditative trance states of various forms.

Some Catholics, like the Warrens (a famous demonological couple), and many Protestant exorcists and demonologists will invite alleged mediums into areas or in the presence of people suspected of being possessed demonically. The idea is for the medium to detect those spirits who are present and hopefully communicate with them in order to either drive them away or find out why they are there. However, if mediumship is real and such an ability to communicate with the dead truly exists in certain human beings, then one is left wondering if such a person, in attempting to communicate with demonic entities, is in great danger of possession or even death via demonic attack.

In regards to demonic possession, the afflicted person may display an ability to communicate with long-dead people. This spiritual communication event has been reported to occur in numerous credible exorcism cases around the world. This seems especially so for human souls that, when physically present, were of the worst character and sinfulness. However, in some cases the possession subject was able to communicate with faithful and loving human souls of some form of relation or another. Necromancy is certainly a sign of possession or demonic influence but could also be the product of mental illness.[4]

19.1.4.4 Remote Viewing

The real-time ability to view a place without actually being there or having any other means of seeing the place is commonly referred to as *remote viewing*. There are many reported instances where a demonically affected person was able to say exactly what was going on in a location that was hundreds of miles away at the exact moment he or she was speaking of it. This ability is considered by many to be included in the *Rituale Romanum*'s listing regarding the knowledge of things that could not possibly be known by the individual without physically being there.

Both the United States and Soviet Union conducted extensive research into the possibility of remote viewing during the Cold War. According to many researchers and historians, the Central Intelligence

---

4. In cases of identified bipolar psychosis, schizophrenia, or other induced state of psychosis in the subject, one should never accept mediumship as authentic in determining whether or not a person is possessed by demonic entities.

Agency conducted years of experimentation with remarkably accurate results. It is said that the Soviet Union's KGB reported similar accuracies in remote viewing experiments. The fact that two of the most powerful governments in the world during the 1980s seriously considered and experimented with remote viewing with some degree of success has lent limited credence to those who believe in it and those who claim to be able to perform remote viewing. However, subsequent research and experimentation has failed to render the same results reported by the CIA and KGB, causing the level of skepticism in this topic to rise substantially over recent years.

19.2 OCCURRENCES AND CONDITIONS OUTSIDE NORMAL NATURE

All experts and possession witnesses agree that demonic possession, especially that which involves the higher demons, is the most bizarre event ever experienced by humanity. Strange is an understatement in describing the incidents and experiences encountered during an exorcism. Everything in nature's way that we have come to see as unbreakable is turned upside down in a case of true demonic possession. Quite literally up becomes down, and what was the rule is no longer the rule. Everything is shaken to its core and redefined, making the very environment of a possession terrifying to those who immediately experience or witness it.

19.2.1 Levitation

The rule is that humans have mass, and mass, in the presence of gravity, has weight. Human weight is always greater per cubic inch of space than air and therefore man does not and cannot float in the air on his own. This is certainly not the situation in many cases of true demonic possession. Under these circumstances, a person, usually the afflicted person, is seen to rise above the floor by as few as a couple of inches to as much as touching the ceiling of the room. If the person is restrained or strapped to a chair or bed then the bed or chair will rise with the possessed subject.

Other items near the possession subject may also be seen to rise and float about the room. This is much different than what is described in telekinesis (section 19.1.2) or poltergeist-like activity (sections 19.2.2, 19.5.1, and 19.5.2) because strictly levitated items seem to hold position or move in a pattern of sorts that rarely result in a "thrown" object or an object that flies from a shelf with force. In this criterion, exorcists and researchers alike have reported furniture and other items as floating circularly around the possession subject. This is sometimes interpreted as a demonic effort to keep the victim separated from human physical contact as would occur in the laying on of hands, anointing of the sick, or in receiving communion.

19.2.2 Poltergeist-Like Activities

The term *poltergeist* originated in the German language and quite literally means "noisy ghost." In cases of demonic possession or harassment, objects are often thrown across the room or furniture may slide across the floor with or without someone sitting in it. There may be scratching or pounding sounds from the walls, floor, or ceiling. Disembodied voices or sounds are also considered to be poltergeist activity and can consist of speaking, screaming, moaning, or even growling in a spine-tingling, beastlike tone.

None of the exorcism cases, determined as most credible, were absent of reported activities of the poltergeist type. Most frequently reported were rapping on the walls, moaning, and beastly growling or snarling. Many demonologists and exorcism experts have asserted the theory that the poltergeists are actually demons in spiritual form causing things to happen in the physical world. Many of the experts seem to prefer the demonic presence theory of the solely telekinetic theory asserted by other scholars and researchers.

Although Anna and Anneliese Michel both reported hearing rapping, banging, and scratching sounds emanating from the walls, no one else in the home reported these occurrences when the sounds were said to have been detected by Anna and Anneliese. Poltergeist activity is very rarely isolated to just the target of harassment or possession and can be heard by all who are with the target or are nearby. Others in the house, such as Josef and Anneliese's siblings should have also heard these sounds, but, as far as is known, they did not report hearing them nor did they confirm Anna and Anneliese's reports of poltergeist sounds.

The recorded exorcism sessions for Anneliese Michel included no sounds of scratching or knocking in the room or in the vicinity. There were also no statements or references by those who were present regarding poltergeist activity during the sessions, either. This absence of poltergeist-like activity tends to lend support to the fact that the young girl was not possessed but mentally ill.

19.2.3 Disembodied Voices Heard by All

Throughout the history of investigated paranormal phenomena, including demonic possession, the experience of hearing voices or screams from entities that cannot be seen is frequently reported. This isn't an event that is reported in all possession cases but certainly is seen in enough of them to justify including it as an indicator of demonic possession. These vocalizations can range from mere whispers to toe-curling screams or wails. They are also reported to range from simple words to complex sentences and even dialogues between the physically living and the invisible source of the vocalizations.

The aggressiveness and vulgarity of the disembodied vocalizations serve to indicate the alignment of the entity that has generated them. If the entity attacks and threatens or uses vulgar expressions, then there is a high certainty that a demonic entity is behind the voices and most likely all other accompanying poltergeist-related anomalies. One must keep in mind that demons, originating in a time many millennia ago, will not speak in modern languages but in the ancient languages with which they are most familiar.

In order for this phenomenon to be recorded as being present, the vocalizations must be heard by all witnesses. These sounds are said to be completely detectible to humans in range of the sounds and will not be heard by only one or two people when there are three or more present. They are also easily recorded by recording devices, and it is strongly encouraged that investigators use such devices in order to detect and record such supernatural events as they happen.

19.2.4 Attacks from Nonphysical Entities

Every reported case of demonic possession and molestation, both credible and exposed fabrication, has included physical attacks on the victim and other bystanders by an entity or entities that were unseen. The results of these attacks include quite visible scratches, cuts, bruises, and red hand marks on the skin. In milder cases, a person's hair might be yanked or they may be pushed or held in place forcefully.

The basic characteristic involved here is actual physical contact between a person and an unseen entity or force that results in clearly visible physiological injury to the person in the form of contusions, abrasions, or cuts. Although many attacks result in no bodily injury, the only useful encounters of this sort are those that can be photographed or video recorded as evidence. Those encounters that cannot be completely documented or adequately documented to support a report of physical demonic attack should be included in narrative reports and witness statements but should not be considered evidence of demonic activity by the investigator. The standard of evidence is too high to allow it for investigative and determination purposes.

Aside from Anneliese Michel's claims of having a heavy weight on her chest during early episodes of epilepsy or even anxiety attacks, there were no other claims of physical contact between her and any unseen entity. The heavy weight experience was felt and reported solely by Ms. Michel, and no other witnesses were available to these incidents. Additionally, Father Ernst Alt and Father Arnold Renz did not record or report any incidents of physical attack by unseen forces against Ms. Michel or any other person involved in the exorcism.[5] There were bruises on the young girl's body, but virtually all of them, especially those around the wrists, torso, and legs, could be forensically linked to the method of physical restraint used by the exorcists and participating family members during sessions of exorcism.[6] The darkening around the eyes can be attributed to two possibilities: either injury during physical resistance or malnutrition.[7]

---

5. In a letter to Bishop Stangl, Father Alt did say that he became instantly nauseated when he saw letters written by Anneliese and Anna Michel. However, this is experienced and reported by the same person in absence of any witnesses, making the claim unverifiable and worthless in an evidentiary capacity.

6. Martin Kehler, postmortem report on Anneliese Michel, July 1, 1976.

7. Benjamin W. V. Voorhees, "Malnutrition," *New York Times Health Guide*, http://

19.3 VIOLENT REACTIONS TO HOLY WATER, BLESSED SALT, AND ANOINTING OILS

A solid indicator of demonic possession is in the writhing fits of anger and agony expressed by the possessed person when sprinkled with holy water or anointed with holy oils. The demon will react with painful screams and howls with blistering blasphemes and vulgarities following each exposure. This is also true for the touching of the crucifix, or any class-one or class-two relic, to the afflicted person's forehead. There is little room to doubt this form of reaction to such holy things as anything less than demonic. However, there is room for fraud and deceit on the part of the allegedly possessed person.

There is no rule that bars exorcists from using the same level of cunning against the devil as what he uses against humanity. In the spirit of this realization, there is a test to ensure that one is dealing with the demonic and not the invention of human imagination or outright deceit. It is of vital importance to perform such a test in order to completely rule out any and all earthly causes for the subject's behavior.

One should prepare two identical bowls of water. There should be no difference between the two bowls whatsoever. In one is placed ordinary tap water and in the other is placed holy water. During an evaluation session, bring in the bowl with the tap water and sprinkle it as a part of the ceremony so that no difference in behavior can be detected by the subject. Later return with the bowl of holy water and again perform the sprinkling in accordance with the proscribed ritual. Record the reactions to each sprinkling.

If there is fraud, the subject will react with fits or screaming to both the tap water and the holy water or may not react to either. In the case of demoniacal possession the exorcist is liable to be laughed at by the demons as they immediately realize that it is not holy water. Regardless, there will be no reaction to the tap water. However, there will be incredible writhing, grinding of teeth, screaming, and other displays of agony and anger as soon as the subject is sprinkled with authentic holy water. This is especially so for water of holy origin, such as water from the Jordan River.

---

health.nytimes.com/health/guides/disease/malnutrition/overview.html?inline=nyt
-classifier, 2007.

This is the exact same case for holy anointing oils, too. The anointing of the subject with ordinary oil, kept in the same bottle and applied in the exact same manner as holy oils will illicit the same reaction as to holy oil if the individual is behaving fraudulently. But, a demon will make all who are present think that the subject's skin will split from the demon's fit of agony and rage when anointed with holy oil and will not react at all when anointed with regular oil.

An observation regarding the exorcism session of Anneliese Michel is that in the recordings and in other documented accounts, the sprinkling of holy water occurred but the girl's behavior remained the same as it was before the sprinkling. This tends to indicate that there was mental illness and severe delusion at work rather than demonic presence, as the screaming and behavior of the allegedly demon-possessed girl would have been significantly different and far worse as the pain of the holy water affected the demon within. Nothing of the sort happened when holy water was sprinkled on her during the ritual, though.

19.4 DEMONIC NAMES AND LANGUAGES

As was previously mentioned, demonologists, theologians, and ministers have hotly debated the idea that demons will lack use of contemporary names and languages. Those who argue that demons speak contemporary languages theorize that demons have existed for millennia and in doing so have learned the languages of the contemporary world. Opponents to that position state that they, the demons, would have such contempt for humanity that learning current dialects and languages would be among the least of their concerns.

The difference of opinion hinges on whether or not demonic entities are exposed to humans enough to learn new dialects and languages or to acquire names of a more contemporary sort. The advocates of modernized demoniacal entities assert the theory that newer languages are picked up naturally by demons as they roam the earth and pass from person to person throughout the ages. Another assertion is that they have the ability to tap the mind, memories, and skills of the mind they have possessed. But, neither idea seems to answer opposing assertions of absolute contempt for humanity being a hindrance to such learning.

Opponents acknowledge the possibility of using the possessed person to communicate but question whether the demon, as an individual, actually learns or acquires modern languages or adopts modern names. Demonic vanity and rejection of all things human lends a great deal of support to the assertion that learning cultural and linguistic practices of the human race is placed at the very bottom of their concerns. Even with the ability to communicate intentions through the mind and mouth of the possessed body, the names will not change over the millennia. This point has yet to be fully addressed by those who believe demons speak in contemporary languages.

There is a third group of demonological theorists who believe that demons don't speak any form of human dialect, ancient or modern. These experts state that demons and other spiritual beings speak their own unique language and it is that language that is of the greatest indication of demonic presence. When demonic or angelic languages are spoken, say the advocating scholars, human beings are utterly at a loss in understanding them. A very small group has agreed that one or more of the ancient human languages may, in fact, be languages spoken by demonic or angelic beings and thus the speaking in ancient languages and use of ancient names would tend to more prevalent.

19.4.1 Demonic Languages

A hotly debated concept in demonic behavior and presence determination is that of the names and languages used by demons that inhabit human bodies. Many demonologists and ministers believe that demons, being creatures of ancient design, creation, and existence speak primarily in ancient languages such as Aramaic, Akkadian (Assyrian and Babylonian), Amorite, Ugaritic, languages of the Canaanites, Phoenician, Hebrew, Latin, Greek, Sumerian, and ancient Egyptian. These experts contend that demonic entities will not be fluent enough nor be motivated enough to speak in any contemporary language such as English, German, modern Arabic, French, Spanish, Russian, or other languages.

However, there are those who resort to mediumship and other unverifiable psychic phenomena to explain how a demon of ancient times, personality, culture, and language would instantly be able to speak and understand contemporary languages. Some say that the entity simply uses the mind of the individual to speak a contemporary language, but this denies the speaking of languages unknown to the subject. Others say that the entities have learned the modern language through repeated possessions, but who learns a language during a violent confrontation?[8]

Regardless of which side of the debate one may stand, the fact remains that the most credible cases of demonic possession or molestation included reports of ancient languages being spoken by the demons through the possessed person. Many writings on the afflicted person's body and on the walls were consistently reported to be in cuneiform or Aramaic text and language. The presence of spoken or written ancient languages is a tremendous indicator of demonic presence. One should be very skeptical of cases where the alleged demons are speaking in contemporary languages.

19.4.2 Demonic Names

There exists a plethora of credible and not so credible books on the subject of demonic names that line the shelves of libraries and bookstores around the world. The reader is advised to conduct his or her own research on the matter and compose a separate list of telltale demonic names. The concept behind specific names of ancient origin and use is the same as that regarding the use of ancient languages. It is believed that real demons, and not those of human imagination, will have names that are ancient in use and origin. This book contains only a few of the many names of ancient origin attributed to the demoniacal realm.

---

8. Many U.S. soldiers fought Germans in World War II, but few, if any, came back speaking German fluently. The same can be said for repeated cases of demonic possession.

Table 3. List of demonic names

Amy	Buer	Gomory	Menadiel
Andra	Buriel	Hagenti	Mephistophilis
Andrealphus	Busyasta	Halahel	Moloch
Andromalius	Cabariel	Halpas	Murmur
Angra Mainyu	Caim	Harlequin	Nephilim
Antaura	Camuel	Hydriel	Nisroc
Armadiel	Carnesiel	Iblis (Devil-Islam)	Obyzouth
Asag	Caspiel	Icosiel	Orias
Aseliel	Ceberus	Incubus	Ornias
Asmodeus	Cesmak	Ipos	Orobas
Astaroth	Choronson	Isacaaron	Padiel
Astovidotu	Cimeries	Kakabel	Paimon
Asyriel	Daeva (Deva)	Kesilim	Raum
Autak	Dalkiel	Kunda	Raysiel
Az	Dantanian	Kunopegos	Sariel
Azazel	Decarabia	Labartu	Satan
Azhi Dahaka	Demoriel	Lahmu	Satanail
Baal	Djinn (Genii)	Lamastu	Udugg
Baalberith	Dorochiel	Lamiae	Ukobach
Balam	Druj	Legion	Uriel
Baphomet	Eligor	Leviathon	Usiel
Baraqijal	Emoniel	Liderc	Uzza
Barbatos	Ephippas	Lilith	Valac
Barbiel	Flauros	Lix Tetrax	Valefor
Barmiel	Focalor	Lucifer	Vapula
Bathin	Foras	Macariel	Vassago
Beelzebub	Forneus	Maklath	Veltis
Behemoth (Devil)	Fureus	Malgaras	Vepar
Beherit	Gaap	Malphas	Vual
Beleth	Gadriel	Mammon	Zagan
Belphegor	Galli	Marbas	Zarika
Bernael	Gamaliel	Marchosias	Zepar
Bifrons	Garadiel	Maseriel	Zotz
Botis	Gediel	Mastemah	

19.5 CYCLE OF DEMONIC MOLESTATION AND POSSESSION

19.5.1 Initial Contact with Victim

The most common form of demonic first contact is through poltergeist-like activity. The word, *Poltergeist*, is German and literally means "noisy ghost." Events such as things moving around the room in plain sight, objects thrown or knocked down, strange symbols or messages appearing on smooth surfaces, and strange noises are just a few of the indicators of poltergeist activity. In very severe cases, some exorcists and witnesses have reported seeing blood oozing from the ceiling and flowing down the walls. This phase may last for as few as a couple days to as long as a year before graduating to another level.

Apparitions are also commonly reported incidents. Indeed, they are also the most alarming. Those who witness them describe them as appearing either fully solid or translucent. Additionally, demonic apparitions are most commonly reported as being in the form of a child, a hideous creature, or some form of ectoplasmic globular form. Other cases include the entity speaking with the victim or making terrifying noises. Usually, physical contact does not occur in the initial phase but has been reported in some cases.

Initial contact activity is also a very limited form of encounter. For the most part, the encounters are restricted to the person selected by the entity for possession or tormenting harassment. This is a critical point for the investigating demonologist as complaints of visitations that are not witnessed by others can indicate the selection of a victim and can serve to substantiate demonic activity. However, one is urged to ensure that these are not episodes of psychosis or otherwise induced hallucinations.

19.5.2 Escalation of Activity

At some point the demoniacal activity will step up to a more intense and physically interactive level. The victim may experience superficial injuries such as scratches or bruises that cannot be explained. The victim may complain about or show directly observable signs of being struck or pushed by an unseen or, in some cases, a completely visible entity. Furniture may move or slide across a room in plain sight of all present without any form of inertial energy application by man or mechanism.

Disembodied voices or terrible growling or moaning noises may be heard by all who are present. In many cases, the voices heard speak in Aramaic, ancient Latin, or even ancient Syrian languages. However, at this point the demon's aim is to break the confidence, faith, and resistance of the victim. The noises or voices will not emanate or originate from the victim at this point.

Violence regarding the throwing of objects will increase, too. Pictures may now fly across the room towards people and furniture may shake wildly. This is especially so for items close to the victim. A chair, occupied by the demonic target, may slide or be violently pushed across the room. People may be roughly dumped from couches and chairs as they are overturned. A rebuke of the demonic entity may result in a mild to moderate physical attack of the rebuking party, not necessarily the victim, by the demon.

The afflicted person's sleep will be disrupted, and interference may occur when eating or performing everyday things. As a result, the person will be irritable, groggy, and weak. He or she may have difficulty in concentrating or focusing on things. However, one must be absolutely certain that these are not the symptoms of mental illness before determining them to be demonically induced. As the person grows weaker, the demon draws nearer to full inhabitation and possession of the body.

19.5.3 Inhabitation and Possession

When the targeted person has reached a certain point of depleted spiritual resistance and mental exhaustion, the demonic entity will then infiltrate the body and begin to manipulate its physical characteristics and behavior. A few experts have expressed a belief that the person's soul is literally ejected from his or her body, but the majority seem inclined to believe that it remains in a suppressed or oppressed state within the body. This state of being isn't always obvious, though.

There are many cases where the afflicted person is reported to have lived a relatively normal life with only a few uncharacteristic traits being detectable. What eventually allowed the detection of a demonic entity was behavior that was utterly out of character for the person. Some of these cases reported that the demon would remain dormant for the most part and only surface when opportunities to commit deeds of great cruelty or evil presented themselves to the demon within. Possession cases of this sort would certainly explain rulers of great heinousness or ruthlessness like Adolf Hitler and Josef Stalin. Many serial killers have claimed this form of spiritual status as reasons for their behavior (such as David Berkowitz, the "Son of Sam").

In other cases, the demon is in full control, and the behavior and bodily characteristic changes are extreme. It is this form of full possession that many Roman and Orthodox clerics have indicated as the most commonly encountered. The Vatican's official exorcist, Father Gabriele Amorth, and other Roman Catholic clerics have likened these possessions to being remarkably similar to, if not exactly like, what is depicted in the movie entitled *The Exorcist* that was originally released in 1973 and is based on the novel of the same name by William Blatty, originally published in 1971. However, there is a long list of clerics, both Catholic and Protestant, who disagree with this descriptive of possession and dismiss the aforementioned movie and book as nothing more than good works of fiction.

A commonly reported trait of full possession with the demonic entity in the forefront is a series of violent bodily actions that result in injury to the person or others. The person will speak with a voice pattern that is foreign to all and in languages long since forgotten. Holy items such as the crucifix, holy water, or blessed salt will send the afflicted person into fits of pain and rage. The person screams obscenities while wailing, moaning, or growling during the reading of biblical passages.

Physical changes of the body are also commonly reported occurrences. The skin may become scaly and turn to a sickening color. The person's eyes may bleed from the tear ducts and even from the nose, mouth, or ears. Some cases include the iris of the eyes changing from their natural color to a hauntingly black color. The fingernails are also reported to grow rapidly and long like the claws of an animal.

19.5.4 Demonically Influenced Behavior

Unlike full bodily invasion mentioned in section 19.5.3 above, demons may choose to simply manipulate or influence the targeted person into desired actions or behaviors. Demonic influence is often described as impulses towards sin or heinous behaviors. Some people, like family murderer Ronald Defeo[9] who killed all six of his immediate family members in 1974, have claimed that demonic entities tormented them and ordered them to kill. In most cases, such claims are nothing more than desperate attempts to evade being held criminally responsible for their own individual heinous acts.

However, there are a number of well-documented cases of demonic influence, and even the Vatican's top exorcist, Father Gabriele Amorth, claims that Adolf Hitler and Joseph Stalin were either possessed or under the direct influence of demonic entities.[10] Recently released Vatican documents are reported to indicate that wartime Pope Pious XII also believed that Adolf Hitler was either possessed or under the influence of demonic forces and even attempted a distant exorcism that was unsuccessful.[11]

19.5.5 *Confrontation and Exorcism*

Confrontation is described as occurring the moment the priest or minister walks into the room and squares off with the demonic entity. This phase is described as existing throughout the entire process of deliverance or exorcism and can last for periods of time that range from a few hours to a few months. The degree of demonic inhabitation and the number of entities present often dictates the length of time consumed by the confrontation phase.

19.5.6 *Demonic Waning*

At some point during the confrontational phase of the possession, the demonic entity will begin to wane or lose the minimum amount of energy required to remain in the body. This development is a critical

---

9. Ronald Defeo was charged with six counts of murder in 1974 and is part of the real-life inspiration behind the Amityville horror story written by Jay Anson in 1977. This written work is considered a hoax by a number of experts and was contested as fiction in a bitter lawsuit that began in May of 1977.

10. Nick Pisa, "Hitler and Stalin Were Possessed by the Devil, Says Vatican Exorcist," *Daily Mail*, August 20, 2006, http://www.dailymail.co.uk/news/article-402602/Hitler-Stalin-possessed-Devil-says-Vatican-exorcist.html.

11. Michael Dubruiel, "Pious XII Attempted Long Distant Exorcism of Hitler," *Annunciations*, August 29, 2006, http://michaeldubruiel.blogspot.com/2006/08/pius-xii-attempted-long-distant.html.

indicator that the breaking point is near. When this phase or condition presents itself, the exorcist or deliverance minister will often intensify the attack in order to maintain the entity's weakness and hasten the arrival of the breaking point phase of the cycle. It is important to press hard, within the limitations of safety and good common sense, in order to deny the demoniacal presence of any opportunity for recovery of energy or strength.

19.5.7 Breaking Point

The breaking point is reached when the same method used to gain control of the victim is successfully used by the priest to drive the demon out. The method mentioned involves the wearing down and constant tormenting of the target. For the demon, the person is weakened and resistance collapses and for the priest the demon is worn down and eventually leaves, as it has been outlasted or divinely counter-tormented sufficiently to motivate its retreat from the body. The exorcist need only push a little more and the afflicted person will be freed.

Throughout the confrontation phase of the possession, the demonic presence is full of angry and violent energy. But, as the course goes on, this energy begins to wane (section 19.5.6) and eventually disappears entirely when the breaking point is achieved by the priest. The signs of this transition can be seen in the contrasting behaviors displayed by the demoniacal presences. At the breaking point, the demons will act as physically and mentally exhausted as the human victim. Poltergeist-like events, attacks of the victim and others present, and forefront presenting of the demon will reduce sharply to nearly nothing.

19.5.8 Demonic Retreat (Completed Exorcism)

The death of the possession happens when the evil entities depart the afflicted person's body. This is a permanent status and by no means temporary. The *Rituale Romanum* contains a warning regarding deceitful practices where the entities will hide or go dormant in order to regain their strength and power over the victim. Thus, this final step or phase occurs only when the entity has been verified as having permanently departed the victim's body. It is essential that follow-up sessions and evaluations occur and that the exorcist remains vigilant in order to ensure that the demon does not regain its strength. The entire cycle will start over if the exorcist is completely fooled by the dark oppressor of the victim.

Conclusion

Ms. MICHEL AND THOUSANDS of others throughout history have suffered and died because of ignorance. Unfortunately, much of this lethal lack of applied common and formal learning has historically come from the ranks of the clergy. Every deacon, minister, pastor, priest, vicar, bishop, and archbishop owes it to God, Christ, and their congregations to ensure that what they do is in the greater interests of God's will and the safety of those in their care. A huge part of achieving this end is to study the elements of both the spiritual and physical worlds.

If one is oblivious to normality in the physical world, how can a priest identify abnormal symptoms that are of the spiritual realms? How can a minister distinguish between ailments of the mind and body and those of the spirit if he or she is aware of only the ailments and torments of the spiritual realm and ignorant of those existing in the physical world? Complete understanding and power over Satan comes from a thorough and well-rounded understanding of both theology and the sciences of the physical world. This is especially so in matters of human behavior and psychiatric health.

For many centuries, religion and science have been adversarial, when in reality they are two halves of a more complete understanding of nature and the divine. There is no doubting that there is an order to nature, as it has observable mechanisms by which it goes about existing. You cannot have both order and chaos or order within chaos. Something is random and chaotic, or ordered and structured, but it cannot be both at the same time.

The simple truth about science and religion is that science explores and discovers what is created and exists while religion venerates and appreciates it, giving thanks to that which created it. God created the universe and all that is in it. God governs how things interact and behave under certain conditions. God brings order to the chaos. Scientists discover these rules to universal order and navigate them to manipulate the natural order of things. Science does not invent the rules or the most basic blocks of matter; it discovers them. Faith and belief are required elements for both religion and science.

Science, then, discovers what God already created, knows, and controls. It defines what exists and the rules by which it exists. It also shows how other things can be made, through intelligent design and manipulation. The more science discovers, the more we stand in amazement at the brilliance, majesty, and omnipotence of the over-all creator.

Religion professes that which has been discovered by the most brilliant minds of science—that there is order to our universe and that this order cannot exist without something sentient creating and controlling it. The creator, God for many of us, has brought order to the universe through design and will. God created the basic elements of matter and energy and set them free to interact within the boundaries of the natural order. Occasionally, God intervened and created things, such as earth and life, in order to achieve divine design and desires. Through both intervention and natural development God created things such as humankind. Thus, when priests say that God created humanity and scientists say humans evolved from lesser beings, they are actually speaking of the same thing. God creates and then lets what is created develop, or evolve, over time.

Science and religion are not independent opposites but elements of the greater truth of reality and the universe. A complete understanding of God and God's universe by humankind requires the acceptance and acknowledgement of both the theological and scientific perspectives. No one can come to know God fully without learning both God's spiritual and physical sides. The adversary of God and humanity takes full advantage of both the spiritual and physical realms to attack, hurt, and destroy.

God created both worlds, the spiritual and the physical, and this is often forgotten or overlooked by well-intended members of the religious and scientific communities. God lives in both worlds, and so does the great adversary, Lucifer. In order to defeat the devil, one must be able to fight a two-front war of the spirit and the body. We cannot remain rigidly fixated on the past; instead we must be flexible and adaptive to the present while preparing for the future.

Bibliography

Barnstone, Willis. *The Other Bible*. New York: HarperCollins, 2005.

Beer, M. D. "Psychosis: From Mental Disorder to Disease Concept." *History of Psychiatry* 6 (1995) 177–200.

Coren, Stanley. "Sleep Deprivation, Psychosis, and Mental Efficiency." *Psychiatric Times* 15, no. 3 (1998).

Dubber, Markus D. *Criminal Law: Model Penal Code*. New York: Foundation, 2002.

Foxe, John. *Voices of the Martyrs: 33 A.D. to Today*. Alachua, FL: Bridge-Logos, 2007.

Frazier, Kendrick. "Commentary: Clear Thinking and the Forces of Unreason." *Skeptical Inquirer* 26, no. 2 (2002).

Goodman, Felicitas D. *The Exorcism of Anneliese Michel*. Eugene, OR: Resource, 2005.

Graham, Billy. *Angels: God's Secret Agents*. New York: Doubleday, 1975.

Guiley, Rosemary E. *The Encyclopedia of Demons and Demonology*. New York: Checkmark, 2009.

———. *The Encyclopedia of Saints*. New York: Checkmark, 2001.

Martin, Malachi. *Hostage to the Devil: The Possession and Exorcism of Five Contemporary Americans*. New York: Reader's Digest, 1976.

Mead, Frank S., S. S. Hill, and C. D. Atwood. *Handbook of Denominations in the United States*. 12th edition. Nashville, TN: Abingdon, 2005.

Pastoral Care of the Sick: Rites of Anointing and Viaticum. International Committee on English in the Liturgy, 1983.

Peck, M. Scott. *Glimpses of the Devil*. New York: Free Press, 2005.

Ratzinger, Joseph C. (Pope Benedict XVI). *Catechism of the Catholic Church*. New York: Doubleday, 1995.

Scott, Sir Walter. *Letters on Demonology and Witchcraft*. New York: General Books, 2010.

Van der Toorn, Karel, B. Becking, and P. W. Van der Horst. *Dictionary of Deities and Demons in the Bible*. Cambridge: Eerdmans, 1999.

Weller, Philip T., trans. *The Roman Ritual*. Vol. 2, *Christian Burial, Exorcisms, and Reserved Blessings*. New York: Preserving Christian, 2008.

Made in the USA
Monee, IL
25 September 2023

43407161R00134